Dear Lisa,

I hope you find some inspiration in here for you.

With Love + Light

Jim Rees

VICIOUS CYCLE

JIM REES

THE EI GURU

THE EI GURU

Publishing

1 The Laurels, Lye Lane
Bricket Wood
AL2 3RR
Hertfordshire
United Kingdom

www.theeiguru.com

ISBN 978-1-80049-445-9

Disclaimer: As the author, these events are seen through my eyes and I appreciate others may see things differently, this book is a personal viewpoint and I in no way wish to cause offence to anyone mentioned.

*A virtuous circle has favourable results,
while a vicious circle has detrimental
results. Both circles are complexes
of events with no tendency towards
equilibrium (at least in the short run).*

WIKIPEDIA

DEDICATION

This book is dedicated to my 4 children, Megan, Elliot, Daisy and Sam who I am extremely proud of in equal measure. I'm grateful for your continued love and support – you've inspired me more than you'll ever know.

I'd like to thank my editor Ian Fitzgerald who ensured I stayed true to my goal of being open to share my truth and to help others see their own vicious cycles.

Also, thank you to Stephanie Hale who gave last-minute editorial feedback.

Also, I shared a preview of my manuscript with a number of long-term friends and business professionals and their feedback challenged my writing in a very positive way for which I'm massively grateful – their insights allowed me to maintain a balance throughout this book: Jo Madcocks, Paris Golden, Stephen Burr, Max Campbell, Maxine Scott, Harriet Beveridge, Sylvana Caloni, Jon Treanor, Jonathan Deeringer, Patrick Autisser, Jon Shubert, Jill Williams, Mark Foster, Robyn Powell, Nick Froggatt, Fred Boethling, Tim Drysdale, Simon Potter, Chris Ray and my cousin Karon Makreil.

Special thanks to Robin Clarke who designed the book cover

TESTIMONIALS

"I met Jim some 13 years ago at an event for a sponsor which Jim was speaking at.

I heard him speak and was instantly engaged. I loved his story, but it was more about his passion for changing the way people think. We chatted after and instantly hit it off ... both having the same passions and energy for life.

Jim is always wanting to help others, so there was only one way he could tell his story, be vulnerable and tell the truth. We have been best mates since that day and my life is richer for it. I'm very close to Jim and know his story really well... But I still get blown away by obstacles he had to overcome as a child and his reflections about how his childhood created patterns for him as an adult. *Vicious Cycle* is a brutally honest story of his journey using his insights and blind-spots to show others what they might be missing and how to see them!

The race is crazy ... but it shows you with the right mind set what can be achieved – but be aware at what cost.

We all have a journey and story: this book may help you look a little more at your own ... it's never too late to try new things."

MARK FOSTER
5-time Olympian. Held World, European and Commonwealth 50m swimming titles and smashed 8 world records.

"Raw, powerful, profound. This is a searingly honest, heartfelt book which inspires the reader to both introspection and action in equal measure."

HARRIET BEVERIDGE
Co-author of *Will It Make The Boat Go Faster?*

"This book speaks to our soul and then looks behind the mirror. A brutally honest and beautiful account of what it is to be human. Insane odds confronted and conquered. Mirrored by relationships that come and go. That is the *Vicious Cycle*."

CHRIS RAY
Former Royal Marine, Professional Triathlete and MD of Vision Performance

"All people have extraordinary life-stories to tell but since I met Jim Rees over 20 years ago I have found his story to be one of the most fascinating. I first engaged with Jim in my work as a Psychologist, while advancing a new concept at that time called 'emotional intelligence'. Characteristically Jim was an early adopter who went on to master the subject and inspire countless others, including myself.

Jim's story is intriguing, not only has he completed the world's toughest ultra-cycling event, but he is one of only a handful of people to repeat the event several times! Which takes us into the core of this book; Why would someone choose to do this? And, What can others learn from it? Having spent his career as a professional coach, forensically analysing the motivations of others, Jim is eminently qualified to examine these questions.

What makes Jim's story special is his authenticity. In this book, he unravels past experiences, explores his vulnerabilities and questions his relationships with the same ruthless honesty and compassion he does as a coach. I thoroughly enjoyed Vicious Cycle which reads with the same contagious emotion and enthusiasm as when meeting Jim Rees in person.

Dr Jolyon Maddocks
Author of *Emotional Intelligence at Work - How to make change stick*

Jim Rees is an accomplished athlete, executive coach and author. His professional career has been focused on emotional intelligence and leadership development. His new book, *Vicious Cycle*, provides a look into the mind of the athlete while he takes on the challenges of the world's toughest endurance race.

Race Across America (RAAM) is a 5000-kilometer non-stop bicycle race coast-to-coast across the USA. Participants and their support crews come from all over the world to participate. In nearly four decades there have been only 347 official solo finishers. Rees has finished Solo RAAM three times, each time improving his performance.

From the initial decision to race to a successful finish, RAAM presents a seemingly endless array of challenges – financial, organisational, physical and emotional. Rees is uniquely qualified to take on these challenges and tell the story. Few individuals are able to objectively look at themselves, question why they make the decisions they do, and make changes that allow them to become a better person. Rees does that. More importantly, he inspires those around him to do the same.

For most RAAM participants, the race is a life-changing experience. Many books have been written about the RAAM experience. But *Vicious Cycle* stands out in that it is a compelling read, offering a unique perspective, by a particularly well-qualified author."

Fred Boethling
President/CEO – Race Across America

"I was a teenager when I first became aware of Jim. Watching the 2007 RAAM documentary left me in awe of the mindset of this indestructible man. I had to meet and learn from him, and that was precisely what I did. Jim has always been generous with his time and encouragement, even for a young man who he didn't know – invariably one of the first to offer words of wisdom when I tackle the biggest challenges in my life.

Jim's book will leave you in no doubt about why he goes out of his way to help those who reach out to him. A gripping, brutally honest and touching account of how a life of adversity and success can be embraced and harnessed for personal growth and the benefit for others. Through Jim's experiences, as well as cleverly selected proverbs and teachings, you will struggle not to walk away from this read, compelled by his story and left profoundly contemplating the positive changes that we can all apply to our lives.

The world needs to read, hear, and be inspired by Jim, a man I feel fortunate to call my friend."

JONATHAN SHUBERT
Round-the-world cyclist and 100-mile cycling world record holder

"*Vicious Cycle* is a powerful, raw script encouraging the reader to recognise and challenge self-limiting patterns.

Jim is refreshingly open and honest regarding his own susceptibilities and significant life battles. He manages to harness his life experiences as a high-performing ultra-athlete and specialist practitioner in Emotional Intelligence to provide expert insight in navigating some of life's greatest challenges.

This is a compelling guidebook to understand the core concepts, importance and power of Emotional Intelligence and is testament to the amazing power of the human spirit in the face of vulnerability.

Emotions play a significant role in individual success and great leadership. *Vicious Cycle* reveals how we can understand and connect with our self-awareness to help us overcome our own damaging self-defeating emotional impulses.

Prepare to be moved, entertained, and expertly directed by a man who has been taken to physical and mental breaking point on his journey. Jim inspires us to redefine our individual capabilities."

MAX CAMPBELL: BA (HONS 1ST)
Leadership & Personal Development, Team GB World Championship Athlete and
Multiple Ironman.

"I first met Jim late in 2016: it was an introduction from a mutual friend and I really met him only as a matter of courtesy. I didn't believe I needed the services of a professional coach, chiefly because I viewed it as an extravagance that was a bit egotistical.

We had a short meeting and although I was sceptical, Jim offered me the first session for free. Being a Yorkshireman I find it difficult to walk past a good deal, so I completed my EI questionnaire and had my results and feedback from Jim at my office in Canary Wharf.

I had a lot to work on! He reflected some patterns I was running which I was either unaware of or had buried.

Since then, I have spent two hours every month with Jim. I think that speaks volumes.

He has influenced me to read and face things that I simply would not have without his support. As a consequence, I have become a better leader and I would like to think a better person. I am so much more aware than I was four years ago and, as a result, my career has progressed well. His influence on me has also helped support positive change for the business I work for at a corporate level.

Jim has become a close friend over that time; we see each other socially as well as professionally. He has also helped me navigate some difficult personal issues over that time.

Having read this book, I can honestly say this is Jim: open, vulnerable, spiritual, kind, generous, compassionate and yet determined to always make a positive difference with whoever he works with.

This book contains so many useful insights and messages for readers, I am sure a spark will be created with readers that leads to personal improvement. Like the spark that helped me four years ago!"

NICK FROGGATT
Area Director – South West & Northern Ireland

"An exceptionally rare and honest account of what it takes to achieve truly extraordinary things. Not just the how to but also the reality of the sacrifices made and challenges faced. An authentic and compelling read."

TIM DRYSDALE
Global Digital Sales Transformation Specialist

"I read *Vicious Cycle* at a time when Jim was not only a mentor for my RAAM journey, but also someone who helped me as a life coach focusing on my awareness of how I interact with the people around me. Jim has been there and got the t-shirt, but rather than shouting about it, he gently guides you through his story and exposes his vulnerability and shares his own insights and reflections. This book will explore success and self-development, while also addressing the importance of our close relationships and how the struggles we all face are what shape us as human beings."

SIMON POTTER
Virtual Race Across the West of America Winner, 2020

When I was done reading Vicious Cycle, I read it again. Raw, gritty, and refreshingly honest, this is not another vanilla self-help book that you read and shelve. Quite the contrary, it inspired me to reflect more deeply on my own patterns (cycles) of behaviour - good, bad, and ugly. Jim's personal story is compelling, and his insightful reflections on his physical and emotional journeys really struck a chord. You don't need to be an elite athlete to appreciate this book (thankfully!), as so many of Jim's lessons and anecdotes are exceptionally candid and relatable. The real power of Vicious Cycle is that Jim brings to bear his rich perspective as an experienced executive coach, and turns this light on his own life in a powerful, vulnerable, and instructive way.

JONATHAN DEERINGER
Owner, Deeringer Wealth Management, LLC

"I have known Jim Rees for many years, I have had the pleasure of working with him on numerous occasions. Jim is a consummate professional who has 'lived through' what he teaches so well. Human development is a triadic interplay between physical, psychological and societal factors. The human life cycle depicts a developmental process through which a person gains the "virtues" or "strengths" appropriate for ever-widening social interactions. Jim skilfully aligns his personal quest to the learnings he experiences in 'Vicious Cycle' that outline this interplay so well. This has informed how Jim has approached his own Emotional Intelligence building it to an extremely high level. How he developed his own 'hybrid' approach to his compelling learning style and approach. A must read."

JON TREANOR
Psychologist and Transpersonal Psychotherapist

"My cousin Jim came to stay with us when he came back from Australia in 1984. He was a pleasure to have around; he helped us with our eating habits and exercise – we needed it!

Jim has always been there for me: when my mum died he was one of the first people to come and see me, he knew just the right thing to say and he was there again when my Dad passed away years later with a long a protracted illness, he was on holiday but it didn't matter. I thought I knew Jim pretty well, but when I read his book I struggled to put it down. I found the stories about the 4 RAAM's all very exciting. He just got on his bike and kept riding, I didn't realise how much went into it. The book also gave me further inspiration for my London-to-Brighton walk and a marathon I've signed up for, so thank you Jim. I was also very sad to think that Jim had been there for me, but I had never been there for him in all his hours of need because he was always busy doing something and always so positive, I didn't think that he would actually need me.

Vicious Cycle taught me to look closer at people and make sure that they are really OK; don't just think of yourself and your own little bubble.

It also helped me look at myself and the patterns that I've run through my own life.

Ultimately, this book deserves to be read by anyone who wants to improve areas of their own lives."

KARON MAKREIL
Proud mother of 4 children and 12 grandchildren

"I have the pleasure of knowing Jim and feel lucky to be able to call him my friend.

Vicious Cycle is a beautiful book packed full of insights and lessons.

Delivered in his signature warm and relaxed style, Jim's willingness to share his vulnerabilities gives you, the reader, the courage to take a peek within your own life and start asking questions.

If you're interested in getting to know who you really are, then you should read this book."

MAXINE SCOTT
Mind, Body & Soul Detox Practitioner, Entrepreneur & mother of two

"Having been a reconnaissance soldier in the British Army for 18 years, completing almost every gruelling course the Army has to offer and with 5 frontline tours in Afghanistan and Iraq to my name, I know a bit about sleep deprivation and physical endurance. To try and understand the impact physically, mentally, emotionally, and spiritually, in a twelve-day sleep deprived race and being in a constant physically-active state is something I cannot comprehend. Jim does a great job of putting us in his shoes, along with his support crew and impact of those closest to him that are affected by such a feat, in the epic Cycle Race Across America.

This book will get you thinking, inspire you to have a deeper understanding of who you are and why you are here. Through Jim's story it has allowed me to not only ask myself questions but guide me towards some of the answers to those deeper, more meaningful questions we should be asking ourselves in life.

Jim came into my life early 2020, with a chance encounter at a local gym we both attended. At this point in my life, I had recently made a conscious decision to be more social and interactive with people I did not know. Jim mentioned the words Emotional Intelligence to me – words even at the age of 34 I had not heard together and after years of severely suffering with Post Traumatic Stress Disorder. These words instantly had a huge impact in to how I conducted myself in every aspect of life and my journey to recovery.

Jim has become a close friend and mentor in the short time we have known each other. He has certainly had a part to play in the founding of a military mental health charity I have founded and helps to be a fount of knowledge as I prepare for a 5,800-mile run around the UK coastline within 200 days.

Paul Minter
Former Reconnaissance Soldier and Founder of Head Up Charity

"In Vicious Cycle Jim courageously explores childhood wounds in his quest to become an even more compassionate and effective father, coach and leader. I felt privileged to witness Jim's extraordinary physical and mental feats and the amazing vistas as he cycled across the vast US continent. In his story he reminds those of us in the helping professions that we need to clear our own issues to avoid projecting them onto our clients. And that with care, commitment, practise and self-awareness we are all capable of making significant shifts in our personal and professional lives."

Sylvana Caloni
Leadership coach and co-author Humble Crumbles

*Discovering who we are will force us to
accept that we can do more than we
think we can, we are only scratching
the surface of our potential.*

JIM REES

FOREWORD

The first time I met Jim Rees was in 2003. One of the benefits of working for a large blue-chip corporation was the number of courses I was encouraged to attend. So, when a programme of personal development training was offered I jumped at the opportunity. It was a few days away from the regular grind, and if I learned a bit about myself in the process all the better. Jim was the course facilitator.

It was difficult not to treat these course leaders with a healthy amount of suspicion. Am I being psychoanalysed? Is my every move being reported back to HQ? Will my body language today result in a cardboard box and a letter giving me my notice waiting on my desk tomorrow? Jim and the other facilitators tried to reassure us that we were in a safe environment, that nothing would be fed back to our bosses. We were more than free, they informed us, to make complete tits out of ourselves in front of our colleagues.

Equally, Jim had to win our trust to ensure we got the full benefit from the programme. He revealed a few facts about himself: born in England and grew up in Australia, participated in Ironman triathlons, had four children (at this point I'm thinking: "he has a very understanding partner"). Throughout the sessions the relationship between facilitator and delegates was no more than courteous and respectful. I enjoyed the course, though, and I didn't make a complete tit out of myself. In fact, I still use some of the tools and materials I picked up to this day. But once it was over we all returned to our day jobs and went about our business.

My next encounter with Jim was as a customer. I had moved on to yet another soulless corporation and found myself in an environment I was not suited to. Frustrated and bored, I took the opportunity to hijack a day at the annual sales conference to try and inject some energy into myself. I rifled my address book to find the training company I had experienced in the past and contacted Jim.

Jim and his colleague delivered an exceptional programme and we all left the venue buzzing with energy and excitement. Unfortunately, for me it had merely re-awakened a sense of what was important in an organisation and I definitely was not getting it where I was. For the first time in my career I felt out of place, unable to connect, unable to make a difference.

Frustration turned to self-doubt. Self-doubt to something darker. Very quickly I was struck with physical symptoms which at the time I could not explain, but in retrospect were very clear signs of depression: insomnia, poor digestion, and all the while the nagging self-doubt and introspection weighed me down.

My wife, Katie, was extremely concerned. We had recently married, were looking to move house and settle down, and now her husband of three months had gone from successful, confident and happy-go-lucky to an emotional husk. She implored me to seek help.

I went to see my GP, who explained the situation to me with stark clarity: "You have depression. I can prescribe you drugs to help. They are really quite effective." I was shocked, terrified and relieved at the same time. Shocked to hear the truth, terrified by what this meant (I was "weak"; I had "failed") and relieved that what was making me so unhappy had finally been identified – and could be treated. In order to process all of this I needed someone to turn to. A neutral, with an objective opinion; someone who would not judge me. Katie suggested Jim.

We met in an overpriced hotel just off the M25. A couple of cappuccinos and a biscuit and not much change from a tenner! I'd expected this to be expensive. One-to-one coaching is not cheap. I explained to Jim how I was feeling, that I needed some guidance and was prepared to pay for it.

Jim flatly refused to accept any money, saying: "One, you can't afford me! Two, this is a pleasure. I'm here on purpose. I'm here to help people and I can help you." I actually found this response extraordinary and somewhat uncomfortable. Here was a guy I hardly knew prepared to invest his time in me and wanting nothing in return.

This was not the sort of transaction I was used to dealing with in the cut-throat corporate world. This gave me my first insight into the DNA of Jim Rees. There was something different going on here.

Over the next two hours Jim asked questions. I cried. I left feeling wrung out. But I had made a start.

Weeks passed and I wobbled my way to some kind of progress. I found a new job, believing that, as a change of job had coincided with my depression, then changing my employment would remove it. Cause and effect, surely? I just had to endure a three-month notice period and everything would be OK again. Simple. Except it wasn't simple. Life was about to throw one huge curve ball my way. A reminder of what is truly important.

Katie was diagnosed with cancer.

She fought it. It was tough. Sometimes unimaginably so. But she beat it. Cancer will always be part of our lives, but for now it is very much on the periphery. For me, it was a stark reminder of how fragile everything can be, how in one fell swoop our lives can suddenly change forever. And how we have to make the most of the precious time we have in life, and extract as much experience and joy from it as we possibly can.

Meanwhile, I had been aware that Jim was planning to enter some crazy cycle race. He had mentioned to me that he and three friends were entering a team in the Race Across America (RAAM). I had never heard of the event and had no sense of the scale of the challenge involved.

I acknowledged that west to east across America was a long way, but my engagement in Jim's undertaking did not stretch beyond wishes of good luck. Jim, though, was eagerly anticipating the race and seemed absorbed by it, as if he was about to embark on a spiritual journey.

I had little understanding of what this meant or what Jim's preparations involved. Caring for Katie and starting a new job amply filled my waking and sleeping hours.

I was mindful to call Jim on his return from America. Expecting to hear tales of adventure and victory, I was taken aback when Jim began to recount his experience. Jim's team, he told me, had been dogged by infighting. The principles and ideals that had bound them as a unit had disintegrated almost as soon as the race had commenced. Despite this, they had finished fourth in the team event. But Jim was visibly distraught by the experience. For him the race had turned into a tortuous journey of team tension and aggravation. This had not been Jim's vision for the race or for the team's legacy. There was unfinished business, and Jim's appetite for RAAM had been well and truly whetted. And I was going to help him to satisfy that appetite.

Paris Golden
Managing Director at McCormick & Company

CONTENTS

Introduction …1

Chapter 1. Unravelling Why … … … … … … … … … … … … 11

Chapter 2. My Path to Ultra-Racing … … … … … … … … … 25

Chapter 3. My First Date with RAAM … … … … … … … … … 35

Chapter 4. Going Solo and Getting to the Start Line … … … … 45

A Different Lens … … … … … … … … … … … … … … … … … 73

Chapter 5. Returning to Solo RAAM … … … … … … … … … 77

Chapter 6. Third Time Lucky? … … … … … … … … … … … 91

Some thoughts from Phil Roberton, Crew Chief for 2009 … … … … 109

Chapter 7. Reflections and Insights … … … … … … … … … 113

Chapter 8. Validation … … … … … … … … … … … … … 125

Chapter 9. What Fingerprint will you leave? … … … … … … … 137

Chapter 10. Bringing it all Together … … … … … … … … … 147

Chapter 11. A Happy Ending … … … … … … … … … … … 153

I CAN'T … … … … … … … … … … … … … … … … … … 161

Outro: Covid-19 … … … … … … … … … … … … … … … 163

Afterword: The Final Say by Craig Harper … … … … … … … 167

Values Exercise: Looking Backward … … … … … … … … … 173

The Handprint Goal Setting Model … … … … … … … … … … 174

INTRODUCTION

I have a passionate belief that everyone on the planet is "Built for Greatness": we have all experienced through history some of the amazing things others have achieved using their inner greatness, some with remarkable results for humanity and some with dreadful outcomes.

I believe we all have that same inner greatness and that it's a seed that's planted there when we're first born. It's our conditioning that either allows it to shine and show up throughout our lives, or our inner greatness can be dampened down by our conditioning, making us believe that we are not worthy and can't achieve great things in our lifetime.

Over the past 20 years I have been privileged to see through my coaching practice just how people have transformed themselves from being down and stuck in running poor patterns of behaviour and not tapping into their inner greatness, to turning it all around and living a more abundant life and being better leaders of themselves, their families and their teams. So I know for sure that it's possible to change your thinking, which in turn will change your behaviour and ultimately your outcomes you are pursuing in life.

My hope is that you can learn from some of the examples I share with you, so that you don't walk down some of the dark alleys I've found myself in at various stages throughout my life, I've also had a lot of spectacular experiences sprinkled through my life. Seeing my children born was one of the most wonderful things I have ever seen and I got to see all 4 of my kids come into the world, the mixed emotion from fear that they are going to be healthy and have all their fingers and toes, to the sheer elation and relief that all is well.

I'm hoping that this book will touch you emotionally and make you think and look at where you are right now in your life, to take a moment and do a stocktake of how you've shown up and what energy you have been transmitting out to the world.

I have a simple model that frames my coaching practice: it's the ABC of Success.

AWARENESS is the key to change and the biggest change we can make is managing our emotional state more effectively – that takes effort and courage. We have a choice to make about how we show up and the energy we cover people with. We all get stuck from time to time but that should only be temporary; we shouldn't stay in a negative state for a day, week, month, year or a lifetime!

There's a scale we use in coaching which is a way to calibrate your emotional state. It's simple: 1 represents a poor emotional state/energy and a 10 is a high emotional state/energy. Unfortunately some people do live their lives playing from a 5 or below, they are literally stuck, what keeps them stuck is their story, the story they're telling themselves about why they can't do stuff.

BELIEF in their story ingrains the way they interact with themselves and the world in general, including other people, its like a set of lenses that they see the whole world through. It's rare for many people to ever really question their beliefs or where they come from, and whether their beliefs are helping them or hindering them in achieving their life goals. Those beliefs shape their identity of themselves and this can stop people from taking any action at all towards their goals if they believe that they aren't the sort of person that can achieve certain things. This then becomes part of their story and reinforces their view of themselves.

COMMITMENT is the final part of the ABC of Success and it's the Achilles heel that stops so many people from achieving their goals. The commitment to seeing something all the way through to completion, and there's an emotional state that you need to tap into to be able to stay on track and focused to get stuff done, it's a 10!

Hindsight is a wonderful thing. Looking back, we can make sense of most things that have happened to us, make the connections we weren't able to make at the time. But the important thing is to have the right mindset and use the learning taken from those hindsights to create better outcomes in the future.

When I look back at my life I'm grateful for all of my experiences, including the unpleasant stuff. Everything I have experienced has put me in a great space to be a better parent, a better coach and, hopefully, a better human being who cares about others.

My early conditioning didn't necessarily set me up for success. I didn't consciously embark on this journey to prove anything to anyone, including myself. It's only on reflection that I can weave it all together and make some sense of what has driven me. What my WHY is.

Doing that work is so tough that most people don't go there, spending time looking at what legacy you want to leave behind takes time and introspection. It's much easier to look for things to blame for us not being as happy or as successful as we want to be. The list is endless when you don't take 100% responsibility for yourself because it helps you to hold on to not having to change anything about yourself.

For me, the Race Across America was going to be the biggest physical challenge. I knew that it wasn't going to be easy and that was why I was doing it. What I didn't know at the time was the invisible force that was driving me to go beyond the edge of what was possible. To test myself, to see if I was worthy of the love from those close to me.

Something deep within me was compelling me to push myself, to see if I'd be able to break myself open and discover who I was and what I was made of.

Was I tough enough?

Did I have what it took to finish one of the most gruelling races on the planet and to race over 3,000 miles across America on a bike within 12 days as a solo rider?

Who would I become as a result of pursuing this goal?

In an attempt to find myself and prove myself, I'd lost some of the people I cared about and loved. This was not about the race or about whether I was worthy, it was about life and finding out the deep-seated values that were missing from an abused, abandoned and adopted little boy, who was searching for answers.

This was a vicious cycle that had been reoccurring for most of my life. Overcoming a race such as this was easy in comparison to what lay beyond the finish line.

I was blindly addicted to proving myself. I didn't realise that all my inner child wanted was to be loved and accepted by others, but that first I had to love and accept myself. Even though I had been able so far to successfully finish the Race Across America four times, once as part of a four-person team and in three consecutive solo races in 2007, 2008 and 2009, going faster each year, I still didn't feel that was enough.

When I eventually looked at myself in the mirror to consider what I had achieved in my relentless pursuit of acceptance, I fell into a deep hole of shame and guilt.

Attempting to create anything from this energy was hard. On the surface, people would see the person I wanted them to see: a happily married, proud father and a successful executive coach. It took so much energy to hide behind that mask I had created for myself because I was afraid that people wouldn't like the real me.

Yet I didn't even know who the real me was. I was happier to hide behind the made-up version. The real challenge was: could I be vulnerable enough to share my deepest fears, my truth and bare my soul to allow others to learn from my insights and to help them see their own inner greatness?

It has taken over ten years for me to sift through and unravel this vicious cycle and discern the patterns of behaviour that were blind spots for me, and then in turn be able to share my insights with you.

The weird thing about the Race Across America is that I never doubted I'd be able to finish it. My belief about being able to punish myself, to do whatever it took to be an official finisher, was a given in my own head. I've always believed I will be able to achieve whatever goals I set for myself. That's always been the case so far.

I might not achieve it on the first time of asking, but I'd always nail it on the next attempt. I don't believe in failure. I stepped up and had a go and learnt through that process of putting myself forward. That scared little boy inside me was so desperate to prove himself that he didn't mind a bit of pain.

In 2007, in search of a deeper and richer experience without all of the drama of managing three other riders and a big crew from the 2005 four-man race, I put my front wheel on the Race Across America start line with the intention of breaking the British record of 11 days and 23 hours set by Yorkshire-born endurance cyclist Chris Hopkinson. I believed that I could do it and set about training during the summer of 2006, whilst at the same time searching for crew members to support me in the race and trying to attract sponsors to bear some of the costs.

I didn't really have a well-researched training plan as such. A friend of mine who knew about ultra-cycling said it was all about getting used to riding on sore legs. Little did I know that there would be a lot more to it than that, or what the universe had planned for me and my ego that year, as well as all of the lessons for me personally and for the crew that were to unfold.

Ultimately, it took me six months to recover physically from the 2007 race. My hands were numb and it continues to be a problem to this day. Even on a ride of a few hours and the numbness will start to come back.

In terms of recovering financially, it's still ongoing. Doing three solo races in a row has had a big knock-on effect on my business, taking my time, focus and attention away from my work. There was also the matter of the global financial meltdown starting in 2008 having a big impact on the area I work in. Training and development budgets were cut, especially for the senior leaders that I worked with then and now.

I'm not complaining. I chose to compete, and did so with the thought that I would be able to share the learnings from my race experiences to help others understand what drives us as human beings to do some of the extreme things we do. Strangely, I got more than I could have bargained for in terms of life experiences.

The emotional impact on my family has been massive. There are choices you have to make in order to compete in this brutal race that require a self-obsessed approach to training and recovery. Something has to give. I made choices that impacted on my ability to be a bread-winner. This in turn impacted on my ability to see my children on a regular basis.

With my rose-tinted glasses conveniently on, I could easily come up with a story as to why it was OK not to see my youngest daughter, for example. She was a teenager with her own life, happier to be with her friends than with her dad was what I told myself.

It really is that easy to catch yourself in a cycle that serves your own goals, and that was the pattern of behaviour I allowed to run in the background whilst pursuing my goal of competing in the Race Across America – a vicious cycle indeed!

The wounds created by this situation will take time to heal. Given that I grew up with a pattern of being abandoned, the vicious cycle has truly been carried forward. My relationship with my kids from my first marriage has understandably taken a long time to heal and it's still ongoing, I deeply regret the poor decisions I made back then.

My leaving and starting a new family was tough for my kids, and I missed them all. What I realise now is the constant battle that I have struggled with which is all around getting a balance of the three core aspects of our lives: self-care, family and career.

We had filmed a documentary of my solo ride in 2007 and this helped more people in the UK to hear about the race. I had already committed to competing again for 2008, as I believed I could go quicker than my official time of 12 days, 4 hours and 52 minutes (8 minutes within the cut-off time). By all accounts this was the closest finish to the cut-off time in RAAM history – I finished with 8 minutes to spare – until the 2011 race, when America's Geoff Brunner finished just seconds within the deadline.

On top of that, I had big plans to take a large RAAM contingent across to do the race. I originally wanted to field a four-man team, a four-woman team and an eight-person mixed team, as well as me riding solo. We ended up at the start line without the eight-person mixed team as we had trouble recruiting a support crew and the finances were way too tight.

Well, talk about looking for different experiences. That year was complete and utter chaos and, without doubt, I took on way too much. When it came time to race, everyone from each of the teams wanted a piece of me.

On top of that, Mike O'Keefe, one of my crew chiefs, had a major health event. He keeled over the day before the race and it was only when we arrived back in the UK after the race that we learnt that Mike had had a Transient Ischaemic Attack (TIA) a small blood clot and could have died.

I did improve on my 2007 time, finishing in 11 days and 8 hours. Yet I still knew I could go faster. My training for 2008 had been slightly different. I had decided to cut out what I considered to be junk mileage, such as training in bad weather. I also knew that I could save time by cutting out what we called "fiddling". In 2007, I'd looked for opportunities to get off the bike as much as possible; the 2008 plan, which we did stick to, was to ensure the only time spent off the bike was for a toilet break or a sleep break. Everything else was done in the saddle.

When we crossed the finish line in 2008, my crew had had enough. We barely celebrated, crashing in our hotel rooms instead for our first decent sleep in almost two weeks.

As for me, I had experienced two very different crews during the second part of the race. The day crew were very gentle, whereas the night crew felt to me like a bunch of bullies. I felt that they didn't understand what I'd been going through, and I was hallucinating badly and felt punch-drunk and drained.

The morning after the race had finished, I began hearing stories from the 4 lady and 4 man teams who'd had lots of issues throughout their respective races, too.

Considering we were all flying under the 'Team Inspiration' flag, it wasn't massively inspirational. It added to the already negative energy from my own race and it was a nightmare that I was very much looking forward to waking up from.

Unfortunately, it's all too easy to forget the great stuff surrounding the race and focus on the negative aspects. It's safe to say I could write another book about how not to do RAAM based on my 2008 race.

In 2009, I was determined to avoid all of the 2008 mistakes. For a start, I wanted the support crew to understand what it felt like to be a solo rider competing in this most brutal of races – so I asked them all to commit to a 100-mile ride at Grafham Waters before we set off for the US.

On the day in question family and friends came along to support all the riders, many of whom hadn't cycled more than 10 miles before. In the end, none of them managed to complete the course. The best crew member managed 70 miles, while the lowest finisher was just over 30 miles. Whatever the mileage, everyone now had some of idea of what ultra-cycling meant.

Or did they?

Despite this, looking back at my three solo races I realise that there's no way anyone can truly experience what it's like to take part in this race as a rider unless you've actually done it yourself; and even then it's still all down to your own interpretation of the events that take place before, during and after the race.

It's taken me years to write about these experiences, as I've been trying to interpret aspects of my own dark journey. I believe we all struggle with dark nights of our soul. They are sent to test us and help us grow, but far too often we don't see them for what they are.

We get caught up in the drama and miss the rich learnings that are staring straight at us. In doing so we drive ourselves deeper into the darkness.

A dark night of the soul can show up in many aspects of our lives: a job loss, for example, a divorce, a falling out with a family member, financial problems, abuse as a child or adult, even the loss of a limb or a long-term injury that prevents you from competing.

It's not always something you see while you are going through the experience; you usually see it afterwards, on reflection – or not at all, unless the pattern is discovered by someone who knows how to navigate their way through these issues.

I've had to dig really deep to help myself understand the vicious cycle that has driven me to compete in endurance races for the past 35 years, and to make sense of other patterns of behaviour that have run through my life and that have not served me well.

I've been lucky to have the support of an amazing friend and coach, Liz Hanson, who was gentle with me while she held the mirror up for me to look at what I had been creating in my life. It's been painful and very insightful, and the work is never done.

This book is my best attempt at sharing my truth with you. Its intention is to help you, the reader, to use your own mirror to see what patterns of behaviour drive you in your life, and to ensure you discover any patterns that are not serving you whilst in pursuit of your life goals.

"Before you judge other people's darkness, you need to become aware of your own inner darkness and deal with it first"

JIM REES

CHAPTER 1

Unravelling Why

I remember my first bike. It was a blue Malvern Star dragster with blue and white streamers coming from the end of the handlebars.

It was an upgrade for my tenth birthday from a two-wheeled scooter, and to me, it represented freedom. I was overwhelmed with excitement when I realised what I had been given. It was by far the best present I had ever received and it transformed my ability to get to friends' houses that were previously too far to travel to by scooter.

From memory, it had four gears on the top crossbar that were like the gears on an automatic car. In those days, you could collect plastic shapes from Shredded Wheat packets and I used these to jazz up my bike, placing them in the spokes to make a distinctive clattering noise, which made me feel as though I was going faster than I actually was.

After school, rides up and down the street with my mates took up most of my time before I would be called in for dinner. In those days, the roads were tarmac but the side of the roads were made up of dirt and chunky gravel.

We would gain as much speed as possible going down the hill and use the gravel as a skid pad to see who could end up with the longest skid mark. As you can imagine, there were a few crashes and it wasn't unusual for me to arrive home covered in dirt and blood after attempting to beat one of my mates.

I would come in screaming and my mum would calmly ask what I'd done this time. She would then set about cleaning the wound with Savlon antiseptic, which would sting like mad. That was only after she'd had a go with a flannel and warm water; getting the gravel out was always the worst bit.

I would never have known then just how large a part bikes were going to play in my life; when I've had periods of not riding, I've felt something was missing. I've never really got on with meditation, but I think it's because cycling is my form of contemplation – you have to be very present when cycling.

It's been my way of clearing stuff and creating clarity. Even though you are moving, you have to focus and be awake to thoughts coming and going, and your awareness is heightened to everything going on around you.

It's been said that endurance athletes are running away from something; for me I think this is true. It's given me the opportunity to hide from the personal stuff I've tried to avoid for most of my life. I've been running away from my inner child whilst competing in Ironman races or training and racing in RAAM. In all that time my inner child never got an opportunity to speak or be heard and my way of dealing with everything was to mangle myself as much as possible so I could dampen down this inner child who only wanted to be loved and understood.

I work in the corporate world as an executive coach and do a lot of one-to-one coaching with senior directors for blue-chip organisations. The core of my focus when working one-to-one with someone is to create a deeper level of awareness for the individual around the foundation of emotional intelligence, which includes having a high self-regard.

In other words, you need to be able to love yourself. If you can love yourself, it's easier for you to love others.

Of course, it's usually the case that people like myself working in this arena have our own issues and this is something I've had to pay a lot of attention to. I had to get to know the inner child that had been screaming at me for years for my attention, but I had ignored him.

I also needed to understand who I was, without the tag of being an Ironman or someone who had finished three solo RAAMs. I had to peel back the layers and make some sense of who I am without all of these labels I was hiding behind. It has been very scary and painful looking in my own mirror, but through that process of self-reflection I have started the healing process which has allowed my deeper personal insight and learning.

I was adopted at 18 months old. I was the second child born into a fairly complex environment. My mother had already allowed my older brother to be taken on by her parents and my brother grew up believing that his grandparents were his parents and that his mother was his sister.

It would be another 35 years before I got to meet my birth mother, Angela King, and find out that I had another half-brother and three half-sisters. And on top of that, a new batch of family. Angela had also adopted a young West Indian girl called Rosie; the pure guilt of giving me up for adoption I believe drove her to try and do some good by giving Rosie a better life.

Angela's story was remarkable in many ways. I believe she was chasing love in all the wrong places. During her first pregnancy she was jilted at the altar by an Irishman who ran back to Ireland, leaving her with a large bump who eventually became my brother Kevin and grew up with his grandparents.

Angela was working in a chicken factory near Twickenham just outside London and was befriended by a lady who was married with two children. She convinced Angela that she could save money by renting a room at their house and occasionally mind her children to allow her and her husband to go out every now and then.

At this stage, Angela was still trying to cope on her own with Kevin, so this seemed to be a good arrangement. There was no way that she could have predicted what would happen next, but life has an amazing way of unfolding!

The woman who had befriended Angela was having an affair with a Lebanese man from the chicken factory and they decided to run away to Lebanon together, leaving Angela with her children to look after and I'm sure a very distraught husband.

You can guess what happened next: Angela and the husband ended up becoming romantically involved. Angela fell pregnant with me and, six months later, the wife returned from Lebanon from the failed relationship and things got very messy.

The husband wanted both women to stay and hoped they could work it out, but Angela, heavily pregnant, ran back to her parents with Kevin and another embarrassing story to tell. This was the early 1960s, when it was massively frowned upon to have children out of wedlock and abortions were rare. So, it's easy to see why Kevin ended up with his grandparents in Tunbridge Wells.

The handover was done under cover of darkness as Angela's parents were too embarrassed to let the neighbours and other prying eyes see what was going on! I'm not sure what story they would have told about the arrival of Kevin to people they bumped into as they went about their usual routine.

Angela ended up going back to Twickenham and found another place to rent whilst retaining her job at the chicken factory.

As for me, my mum was doing her best as a single parent, but the straw that broke the camel's back happened when I was 16 months old. The story I've been told is that when my Mum came to pick me up one afternoon from the childminder's, she noticed that my back and legs and body were covered in bruises.

Apparently, I'd been left in a cot for most of the day and, whenever I cried, I was hit. Feeling unable to cope and filled with self-loathing, Mum looked for advice from social services. The result was that I was put up for adoption, a process that was much easier back in the 1960s. That's how, after a simple court hearing, I went from being Sean King to James Rees.

My new parents, who I called Mum and Dad, had an amazing record of fostering children. They had already adopted two older boys and, though in their mid-40s, were allowed to adopt me. When I was four years old we became some of the last "ten pound Poms", Brits who were encouraged to emigrate to Australia on board the Arcadia ocean liner with tickets costing just £10 per family. Almost one million British citizens relocated down under in this scheme promoted by the Australian government in the 1950s and 60s.

Oddly, I have no memory of the trip. I look at photos now but have no connection with the little boy in them who seemed to be very excited to be setting sail on such a huge ship.

Reading between the lines of the various stories I've been told, we went in order to escape the bailiffs who had been after us for unpaid rent and other bills. Dad had been giving Mum money to pay the rent, but, funds being short, she had spent it instead on feeding and clothing her three boys.

Growing up in Australia was the best thing for me. I was a sporty boy and the weather was great for playing endlessly with my mates. I grew up in a suburb 30 miles outside Sydney called Lidcombe. On sports days, I'd take part in most events. I'd run the 100, 200, 400 and 800 metres and be part of the relay team as well.

On top of that, I'd do the long jump and the high jump too, and compete in most of the distances and strokes at our swimming gala.

In the school holidays it wouldn't be unusual to be out all day exploring the local cemetery (one of the biggest in the Southern Pacific) looking for blue-tongue lizards and snakes, or just out exploring the open sewerage networks. These were huge tunnels that went underground for miles and we would take torches and dare each other to walk all the way through the system.

We also did all the normal stuff, like going to the local pool or the occasional long journey on the train for a day at the beach and all the other things young kids do when they have the freedom or lack of parental control to stop them. We'd play paper chase, and when we got bored with that or it was just too hot to run about we'd climb trees that were three or four storeys high and try to hit each other with a rolled-up newspaper. Kids!

I still can't believe we used to do that and that no one fell out of one of the trees.

During the winter I'd play football and in the summer I'd play cricket. I still have fond memories of all of those times I had with my friends.

I was seven when I was told that I was adopted.

It was the first time I'd seen my Dad cry when he told me that. Because they had chosen me as their son by adoption, it meant more – knowing that they went out of their way and deliberately chose me as their son.

I wasn't upset by this news. I thought that it was pretty cool and I told all of my mates at school the next day. I'm still extremely grateful for having been adopted and it's difficult to imagine what my life would have been like if I hadn't. But that's a whole other story.

When I was ten years old, I was sexually abused on different occasions by people I trusted. It scarred me and created an awkwardness that stayed with me until, as an adult, I was able to internally forgive both of my abusers.

The little boy this happened to is the boy who has wanted to be loved and understood all these years. It's been one of the factors leading me to push myself to near-physical destruction in an attempt to bury my embarrassment and clumsiness.

I realise now that those experiences could have easily turned me into a complete wreck. Instead, it created in me a bullet-proof ability to be able to handle pressure or pretty much any stress. It sculpted a deep emotional resilience that still serves me well today.

I think if I wasn't such a sporty little fella growing up, I might have struggled with having been adopted and sexually abused, but I was fairly popular at school and the outdoor life suited me. It's interesting to reflect that maybe sport was my way to escape and that pattern obviously grew as I got older, it just became more extreme in its duration as I turned away from team sports to ultra-racing.

At 15, I'd had enough of school. My main interest was sport and I found most of my classes couldn't hold my attention for very long. I chose to quit before completing my leaving certificate and started working as a storeman for a pharmaceutical wholesaler. It was the first job I went for and I got it!

I was the youngest buyer in Australia and I absolutely loved my new role. I was being wined and dined by the national sales managers of the big pharma companies and I learnt very quickly that I had a knack for closing big deals – especially when it came to the end of the quarterly sales cycle and they needed me to order more of their products to help them out.

I'd had to convince my Dad that I was old enough and man enough to leave. To see if I was, he challenged me to go to town and buy him a couple of bottles of beer from our local off-licence. Luckily, our family spent a lot of time in the town pub, so I knew everybody that worked at the off-licence and was easily able to complete my task.

Mission completed, I took the next day off school and started looking for a job.

After just six months as a storeman, I was promoted to Ethical Buyer. This meant I was responsible for ordering and keeping in stock the thousands of pharmaceutical products that we supplied to our chain of chemists across New South Wales.

As a young boy with a bit of money in his pocket, I was having a great time. I hadn't even turned 16 yet and had moved out of home and was renting a flat with some friends of my eldest brother, Derek.

Coincidentally, my two older brothers had both left home before they were 16, too.

The main reason I'd left was because of an argument I'd had with Dad. I'd met a girl at Chem-Buy Pharmaceuticals and we started going out. Dad didn't like her, and after he called her a slut I took offence. We were together for four years, but eventually she left me for her ex-boyfriend. After that, I jumped from relationship to relationship, looking for a fairytale romance that was always out of reach.

I think I was looking for someone who would love me from that very first encounter right through to my adult life. I've always had a romantic view of relationships and I believed it was important to find someone who loved me, get married, settle down and build a family. The driving force behind this thinking was my upbringing. I was heavily conditioned into thinking that this is what you had to do, and subconsciously, I was always looking to settle down.

When I was 19, back in 1982, I had an opportunity to travel to Europe with some close friends and decided to fit it in with a one-week trial training with Tottenham Hotspurs reserves. After the trial it was obvious that I wasn't going to make it. I had the fitness but didn't have the ball control and my skill set wasn't to the high standard required to compete at that level.

Once I had travelled around Europe for a few months, I flew back to Oz and started a new job working as the assistant manager at Dalton Pharmaceuticals and met John Ross and his wife Pat. John was the manager of the branch at Penrith and we became close and started competing in 5k and 10k road races on the weekends and eventually did the famous City to Surf fun run.

This is really where my journey into triathlon, and ultimately, RAAM began.

I spent a couple of years at Dalton Pharmaceuticals before I got itchy feet and a deep urge to find out what it would be like to actually live in England – the country my parents had fled in search for a better life –had an invisible pull on me. I was curious to know about my past and where I came from.

At the very core of my inner struggles I was attempting to understand my identity, where I came from and where I belonged. It's the classic questions we all ask ourselves at various points in our lives: why did I show up here and what am I here to do?

I remember my Dad asking me to help him trace his family tree and how excited he was about finding the coat of arms for the Rees name. It was probably the first time I felt a little awkward about not belonging and not really knowing where I came from.

Until that point, I had never really given it much thought.

By that stage in my life I had traced and met my birth mother, Angela King, but hadn't been able to trace my father.

All these thoughts were churning over and over in me – then and later. I was looking for love and looking to be someone's hero, their knight in shining armour. Later, as an adult, I thought the way to do this was by competing in extreme races. But, as much as other people would look on and say how impressed they were with what I had done, it was never going to win over the one person I wanted to win over.

I met my second wife in 1998, when she joined Royce Pharmaceuticals, a company working for AstraZeneca supplying contract representatives and managers. Tracey had just returned from Australia with her husband and two daughters after failing to settle following their emigration to Perth. I was married with three young kids myself and didn't think of her as anything other than a colleague. I eventually became her mentor when she joined the management team and it wasn't long before we both realised we were in relationships that weren't working for either of us.

We were together for 17 years, but, ultimately, the man I thought I needed to be was not the man she wanted. What she wanted was for me to be the breadwinner, someone that would take care of the family; whereas I wanted to be her knight in shining armour, my version of slaying the dragon, was to try and impress her by competing in ultra-races. I can see it clearly now: how can slaying the dragon ever pay for the upkeep of the castle and feed the kids?

But there was a chink in my armour. Ultimately, that chink helped me to identify one of the patterns of behaviour that made it impossible for me to have the relationships I wanted with the people I loved. But that was only after we had parted ways.

I came to know that what I wanted was to leave a positive fingerprint with everyone I interacted with. I believe that in every encounter we have with another person there's an opportunity to leave them in a better space than they were before that interaction. That's what a positive fingerprint is: an impression that is unique to the person that leaves it. I was striving to be the normal guy people could relate to, who went out and did what most people would consider impossible or not achievable for someone who wasn't an Olympic athlete or professional cyclist. The normal chap who had a mortgage and children like most other people.

I also wanted to prove to others that life deals us some tough stuff but it's what you do with it that shapes you into the person you become. I believed that I was making the right choices with all of the right intentions, but, along the way, due to my lack of awareness, I hurt the people who were dearest to me.

The strange thing is that everywhere I look in my life I have re-created the same vicious cycle of being in fear of abandonment, and not just in myself. My eldest daughter Megan from my first marriage has developed the same fear because she remembers how terrified she was at ten years old when I abandoned her and my two other children when I left the marital home. This continued to be an issue in her relationships because she came at them from a place of fear that any new boyfriend would eventually abandon her. This caused her to overcompensate and it always ended in her pushing the boyfriend away because she was trying too hard. The good news is that my daughter has done a lot of growing up and is now more aware of this pattern than I was at her age, and her relationship with her fiancé is strong.

Our lives tend to give us not what we want but what we need to grow and develop. You end up staying stuck if you aren't aware of the patterns of behaviour in your life. All that was ever happening in my life was a repeat of this pattern showing up in different situations. I could do great work with a client and get amazing feedback on the programmes that I had run but then get no further work from them, all of which was part of this vicious cycle.

Ultimately, we all want to be liked and loved. But liking yourself first is key. I thought that I was OK with myself, warts and all, but what was actually going on was very different.

I had found a way to hide my inner child, or my dark passenger, for want of a better description. I dampened down my inner child by being busy competing in endurance races around the world. I was looking to create an identity that I could hide behind and hoped that others would be happy when they met me and spent some time around me. Little did I know that deep, deep down, I wasn't really comfortable with myself.

Pink Floyd wrote a double album called The Wall which was all about how Pink's parents built a wall around their son in the hope of protecting him from the world. My subconscious had been busy building a wall around myself in the hope of protecting me from the same things that the world throws at us. Yet the wall that I had built wasn't serving me well. The wall was so high and so well-built that I couldn't see through it or over it. Ironically, it was the work I do as a coach that led me down the rabbit hole and put me on a path to help me to discover the real me once all of the layers of bricks had been removed. Underneath it all was the scared, vulnerable little boy who was in fear.

Luckily for me, 20 years ago I changed careers and fell into coaching and that new path sent me on a quest to understand myself. In that search, I've been on dozens of courses with various thought leaders and gurus from the spiritual world, all of whom challenged my beliefs about what I thought was possible and expanded my thinking about what one person could achieve and the impact they could have on the planet.

I hadn't even been thinking about becoming a coach. I had spent the previous 15 years in the pharmaceutical industry in sales and sales management. Following my first divorce I moved from Yorkshire down to London and was hoping to find another job in the same industry. That didn't happen. A close friend and previous management colleague at AstraZeneca had left a couple of years before and pursued a career as a speaker and coach and was now working for a large coaching company called Speakers International and there was a job going for an Account Manager, basically a role as a sales person selling high-end corporate change solutions.

So, after an initial meeting in the local pub with two of the principal leaders, I was offered the job! Over the following few months I overcame my fear of cold calling senior leaders and was performing well in the high-paced environment that was just part of the culture at Speakers International.

I became one of the first to transition from sales into coaching as I found a lot of the material and models that we were sharing with clients similar to how I viewed the world. Within three years, I had decided to leave to start my own business as an executive coach and speaker.

There are so many "normal people" who are in a similar place to me. They are out there doing amazing things, such as running 10, 20, even 50 marathons back to back, or swimming mad distances or climbing the world's highest peaks in record times. All of them, like me, are attempting to wake others up, so that they start believing in their own inner greatness so that they too can achieve great things with the right mindset.

My early conditioning didn't necessarily set me up for success. I didn't consciously embark on this journey to prove anything to anyone, including myself. It's only on reflection that I can weave it all together and make some sense of what has driven me. What my WHY is.

Doing that work is so tough that most people don't go there. It's much easier to look for things to blame for us not being as happy or as successful as we want to be. The list is endless when you don't take 100% responsibility for yourself because it helps you to hold on to not having to change anything about yourself.

"A person often meets his destiny on the road he took to avoid it."

JEAN DE LA FONTAINE

CHAPTER 2

My Path to Ultra-Racing

I don't know what it is that drives other men and women to push themselves to near-collapse by competing in extreme races. I do know what it is that attracts me to compete: it's the simple idea of seeing how far I can push myself. It's that curiosity of exploring how close I can get to complete meltdown and still be able function and be able to move forward and be present, to explore how that feels and attempt to understand what is going on in my head whilst everything is happening.

I'm not sure whether it's because of the chemical cascade going on inside you at the point of near-collapse, but I have found myself having almost out-of-body experiences where I become the observer, watching myself riding my bike. I know I'm not hallucinating, I'm more present and aware, it's more like a daydream and it is very peaceful. I'm sure other ultra-racers know what I'm talking about here. I get to a place where I just surrender to everything and accept and enjoy the conditions that surround me at that moment: the weather, the mountains. Any physical or mental issues I have just melt away.

One of the earliest recorded instances of someone pushing themselves to physical extremes came at the battle of Marathon in 490BC, when an invading Persian army was defeated by the much smaller force of Athens. One messenger, legend tells us, was tasked with returning to Athens to bring its citizens news of the battle's outcome. His name was Pheidippides and he ran all the way back to the city, a distance of 26 miles. On arriving he announced "Nike!" ("Victory") and fell dead from exhaustion. Now that is extreme!

Almost 24 centuries later, in 1896, the first modern Olympic Games were held in Athens. The French historian and linguist Michele Breal proposed re-enacting Pheidippides' legendary run in an event that would test man's powers of endurance. The idea was embraced by Baron Pierre de Coubertin, the founder of the modern Olympic Games, and Dimitris Vikelas, the Greek scholar and first president of the International Olympic Committee (IOC). Fittingly, the winner of the first Olympic marathon, which was run from the Marathon Bridge to Athens' Olympic Stadium, on 10th April 1896, was a Greek native, Spyridon Louis. His time was 2 hours, 58 minutes and 50 seconds.

My 1st marathon was the famous London marathon in April 1985: it was meant to be Gary Rogers competing but he had injured himself and I ran under his name, I think the longest run at that time for me was 2 laps of a hilly 10-mile run around Box Hill in the leafy environment of the Surrey hills. The London marathon was really well-organised and had already become a popular event for people around the world and given that it was around some of the famous and treasured sites, including running past Buckingham Palace before you finish, it was really well supported by friends and family. At that time, I was staying with my cousin Karon and her husband Rich with their 2 young boys in a flat in Hampton Wick which was just near the main A3 road into London.

Karon was a hairdresser and was more than happy to put highlights into my shoulder-length hair, I already had fair hair but Karon's highlights enhanced my blonde look. Haircuts for me back then represented a bit of freedom, it reminded me of the lack of choice I had as a boy growing up. Back then, I had 2 choices. My Dad would literally put a pudding bowl on my head and would cut around it to keep a straight line. This resulted in all my mates at school knowing full well that I had a pudding cut and were unrelenting in taking the piss out of me until they had someone else to make fun of, which usually lasted for a good week!

The other option was the classic short back and sides at the local barber's shop. This was almost just as bad as a pudding-bowl cut because the hairstyle back in the early 70s was certainly longer than a short back and sides cut! Of course my so-called mates would rip into me about the shorter hairstyle just as much as the pudding cut! It's funny now but it wasn't fun being that little kid who wanted to be part of a tight group of mates. The only good thing was that it was only ever temporary until the hairstyle settled down and they got tired and moved onto their next target. Kids hey!

The marathon itself is a bit of a blur memory-wise apart from the tremendous support from the crowd – even when you're on some of the more remote parts of the course, people are there cheering you on. I do remember hitting the classic wall that most runners hit when competing in a marathon. This is usually down to the lack of proper nutrition or under-training. It was a lack of nutrition on my part: at mile 18, my pace slowed significantly and my legs were heavy; I grabbed whatever was on offer on the aid stations and hoped that it did the trick of reviving my energy levels. By the time I reached the 20-mile marker, I had 40 minutes to run the last 6.2 miles to break what most would consider the magic 3 hours for a marathon!

I started to feel good again and with my innate competitive nature, I pounded across Tower Bridge and, as I came running down towards Buckingham Palace, the crowd pulled me towards the finish line that I was now completely tunnel-focused on. I could see the finish line and, as I got closer, I could see that I would just miss out on breaking the 3-hour barrier by 1 minute! Still, I was chuffed to bits with finishing my first marathon with a respectable time of 3 hours and 1 minute, I felt OK but after a few hours of walking about and cheering other finishers on, I started to seize up.

By the time I got home, I was hobbling about like someone treble my 22 years of age! The next day was worse, as all of the lactate acid that had built up during the race felt like cement in my legs and it hurt to walk and get up out of a chair! Somehow, it was the day after the day after that was even more painful, it didn't seem as though this was going to get any better at all!

Eventually, the pain faded and the medal and memories of the day washed away the idea of it being a big deal in terms of the pain that needed to be overcome.

Triathlon's roots can be traced back to 1974, to Mission Bay, Southern California, where a group of friends began training together. Amongst them were runners, swimmers and cyclists, and before long their mixed training sessions turned into informal races. Directed and conceived by Jack Johnstone and Don Shanahan, the first Mission Bay Triathlon was held on 25th September 1974 and featured 46 athletes.

Just four years later, in Hawaii, an argument between several athletes broke out following a number of beers about which of the three triathlon disciplines required the greatest endurance. At that time, Hawaii was hosting the Waikiki Rough Water Swim (2.4 miles), the Oahu Bike Race (112 miles) and The Honolulu Marathon (26.2 miles).

Originally run as events in themselves, they were rolled into one and it was agreed that the winner would be called an Ironman. The first Ironman event attracted 15 athletes, with 12 ultimately crossing the finish line. The winner was Gordon Haller, a 27-year-old Navy communications specialist, in a time of 11 hours, 46 minutes, 40 seconds.

By 1982, the Hawaii Ironman challenge was covered on ABC's World Wide Sport programme and featured 580 competitors, the dramatic finish of Julie Moss who had been leading the woman's race all day catapulted the popularity of Ironman around the world. Julie eventually finished in 2nd place after collapsing hundreds of yards from the finish line and whilst she crawled to the finish line was overtaken by Kathleen

McCartney who wasn't aware of Julie's struggles. In 2018, more than 3,000 athletes completed the gruelling challenge. The fastest women finished the course in just under nine hours, with the fastest men finishing in just over eight hours.

Ironman has become a global brand, with the world championships held in Hawaii every October and most other countries also staging events. Triathlon initially attracted marathon runners looking for new challenges and who were tired of picking up niggling running injuries from high-mileage training. The idea of becoming even fitter with less running miles and the challenge of undertaking three disciplines was a major draw.

My route to Ironman competition was different. I was a football player who did fun runs in the off-season to maintain my fitness levels. I eventually gave up playing football age 19 after my one-week trial with Tottenham, so I went back to Australia and started to run more and do more fun runs. Most of these were 10km events, and it was at one of these where I came across someone handing out leaflets for the Nepean Triathlon. My boss John Ross, who had become a bit of a father figure and a mate to run with and compete in all the fun runs together, decided that it would be a great idea to do it, and that's how I caught the triathlon bug in 1982. I remember very clearly after that 1st Nepean Triathlon, we were all completely shattered and sharing our stories of how each of our races unfolded that morning over an Aussie BBQ and a few beers.

We started talking about just how insane it was that people were racing Ironman distances around the world and a number of us, myself included, said that we gave our mates permission to slap us if we ever started considering doing an Ironman race!

It only took me three years to step up from the shorter Olympic-distance races to the Ironman distance. By 1985 I was ready to compete in Hawaii itself, which by this stage was hosting the World Championships for Ironman, it was and still is a huge goal for anyone racing Ironman triathlons to compete against the best of the best triathletes on the planet.

Back then, European athletes didn't have to qualify. I had already moved back to the UK in 1984 and, through an advert in the Serpentine running magazine, I not only found a new friend, I also found someone who was crazy enough to take part in the Hawaii Ironman too.

I decided fairly quickly that I would train with Gary Rogers and from that first bike ride we were almost inseparable. Gary's plan was to over-cook all of the distances as part of our preparation for Hawaii, so we did the Paris-Roubaix Audix event, which was about 180 miles, including all of the cobbled sections! I punctured at least three times and had to ride the last five or so miles on a flat tyre to finish.

Gary had bonked (ran out of energy, a cycling term) earlier and, apart from marathons we ran together, it's the only time I ever beat him as he's usually a better swimmer and rider. I was always catching him on the last leg, the run, but would run out of road. It was never long enough. Even in Hawaii we were only a couple of minutes apart overall, with the advantage to the better biker again.

In the lead-up to the Hawaii Ironman, we ran from my place in Hampton on the hottest day in June 1985 all the way down to Brighton, both of us carrying backpacks with various treats to fuel ourselves and stopping at service stations for top ups. With about 5 miles to go at the end of this epic run to Brighton (which was a place that I hadn't been to before), Gary was slowing down from blisters on his feet, and I was getting fed up and kept on asking that child-like question of "Are we there yet?" Gary's response continued for a couple of miles which was "It's around the next corner," but around each next corner was another long bit of road in front of us with no sea in sight!

I got so fed up that I just ran quicker and pulled away from him and we saw each other again when he turned the final bend in the road and slowly came to a stop at the beach which was completely packed with families enjoying the hottest day that year!

I'm sure this served us well for what was to come in the extreme heat and humidity of Hawaii.

We also both started the South Downs run, which was 80 miles of non-stop running. Gary pulled out at about 38 miles and I continued on with a small batch of other runners going at a similar pace. I remember being lost on top of a large hill looking for a series of white pegs in the middle of the night that were there to help us to navigate. Due to heavy fog, we spent at least an hour walking up and down various hills searching for these pegs. Eventually someone found them and we were back heading in the right direction and I finished in 17 hours and 53 minutes. The scene at the finishing hall was carnage. As the runners shared their stories, I saw some of the biggest and most gory blisters I have ever seen.

When we arrived in Hawaii the difference in temperature hit us straightaway. It was ridiculous to even think about racing in such weather, but that's what we were there to do. I met a fellow competitor called Scott Witter who was working at the airport and we ended up becoming friends and sharing accommodation on the Big Island. Scott showed Gary and I around some of his favourite bike rides and also convinced us to take part in the Tantalus 10, a race that was 5 miles up and 5 miles downhill. A beast of a run. At that time in my triathlon career my strength was in running and I found myself in the lead at the top. Yet part way down the other side, the eventual winner came flying past me. I held on for second overall and, importantly, I'd had my first taste of what it felt like to race in the heat and humidity of Hawaii.

The Big Island experience from start to finish was amazing. I still hold fond memories of the race, the training we did the week before the race and the friends that I still have.

On one of our training rides, the wind was so strong that we ended up riding in single file. On one of the undulations, a friend who was at the front stood up out of his saddle without any warning, causing him to slow his pace. I clipped his back wheel and ended up doing a Superman dive onto the side of the road covered in hardened lava. It was like falling onto really coarse-grain sandpaper and it ripped a lot of skin off my right shoulder. It reminded me of those days as a young kid when my Mum had to clean out all the grit, only this time it was Gary taking great pleasure in telling me to stop moaning. Luckily, the sea water cleaned and healed my shoulder prior to the race start, but I still have the scar on that shoulder!

Gary and I both had amazing races for our first Ironman experience. He got me again by a couple of minutes. Had the run been two miles longer who knows what would have happened!

I competed in 14 other Ironman races around the world after I finished Hawaii in 1985. The following year I flew to Auckland New Zealand in March and did the Ironman race there and then flew over to compete in the Japan Ironman in July. Japan was by far the best result I had achieved in an Ironman race as I finished 19th overall out of 650 competitors. I was the first amateur and 3rd European overall and this was a tipping point in my Ironman career. I was 23 years old and didn't have a structured training plan or a coach at the time. So this was one of those sliding doors moments, where, had I chosen to focus on Ironman triathlons, I may well have made a career from travelling around and competing in Ironman races, but that didn't happen.

I was knocked off my bike later that year cycling to work along the A3 just outside London. A bus full of school kids was turning in front of a large queue of traffic to drop the kids off at the Richmond swimming pool. The bus appeared from nowhere across my bit of road and I came to an immediate stop. Squashed and unconscious against the side of the bus near the front door, I know what the school kids were thinking when they were clambering over one another to get a glimpse on me in a mess on the floor: they thought that the driver had just killed a cyclist!

The accident didn't kill me but it killed off a career in triathlon as it was at the hospital that I met my 1st wife Tracy who was a student nurse on the mixed male ward –and before your mind wanders off with thoughts of bed baths, it didn't happen!

So, as I've mentioned previously, we're all conditioned from our early childhood. Part of my conditioning was that I believed that it was important to meet a girl, settle down and then get married and have kids.

Well, that's what happened. Tracy and I dated for a couple of years and we got married in July 1989, quickly followed by the birth of our 1st daughter Megan in 1990 and followed on by our son Elliot who was born in 1992.

By that stage, just before my 30th birthday, I was already on the treadmill pursuing a career and attempting to support my young family – typical of the pattern I see in a number of the executives I've coached over the years. I too was running the same pattern as a young father. I was chasing a career and looking for opportunities for promotion without thinking of the impact that moving our young family around the country would have on all of us.

This was another blind spot for me: I thought I was doing the right thing by my family by getting the next job that paid better money as I climbed the corporate ladder.

Not only did it place a load of stress on the kids having to move schools and make new friends, it also had an impact on Tracy in the same way as she also needed to embed herself in a new community. With a young family I found it tough to find the energy to get out and go for a run or bike ride due to the long days of travelling around a large area of the country managing a team. This took its toll and over a very quick period and I started to pile on the pounds.

I'm not blaming the lack of a sporting career on being married and having kids – these were all choices I made. Or was it my conditioning that made the choices for me?

Either way, I wouldn't change a thing because we ended up with our 3rd child Daisy born in Yorkshire after yet another career move in 1996. It's beyond mad now I look back at all of the moves and upheaval I put our family through, but as I said it was a blind spot and I wasn't aware of the impact it was having until it starting unravelling due to the strain it put on our relationship as a couple.

I cherish all the memories I have stored with the kids growing up and now realise with hindsight that being a great parent is the most important job we have. Blink and they've grown up!

*"If you think you can or if you think you
can't, you're probably right."*

HENRY FORD

CHAPTER 3

My First Date with RAAM

When I talk at conferences and share some of my experiences from RAAM with audiences, regarding the huge distances covered per day, the extremes of hot and cold temperatures, the sleep deprivation and the hallucinations, I realise that they just can't get their heads around the stats. Climbing 110,000 feet, crossing the deserts in the heat of summer, and the sheer boredom and wind across the plains of Kansas whilst surviving on as little as 60 minutes sleep per day – with even less for the top riders. It's mind-boggling for most people.

The biggest realisation I had recently was when I mentioned to an audience that, prior to RAAM, I used to compete in Ironman events. I saw people visibly become animated. "Wow," they'd say. "You've done an Ironman."

This reaction tells me that people just can't compute the details of a race that goes from Oceanside, California, to Annapolis, Maryland, and covers just over 3,050 miles of non-stop cycling as a solo rider. They don't seem to be aware of just how far that is, or, indeed, what the Race Across America itself is. I too would have struggled with someone describing the event prior to competing in it. I certainly would have said there were a few links missing from their chain-set, or, better still, get the men in white suits to take them away.

Ask most people to name a bike race, they will almost always say the Tour de France. The most famous and prestigious Grand Tour has over 100 years of history and attracts over one million spectators along its route, plus a global television and internet audience of up to 3.5 billion viewers. The three-week event is a moving masterpiece on two wheels, set against a backdrop of breathtaking beauty and bonhomie that is quintessentially French.

Almost 200 of the world's greatest riders compete in the athletic and tactical battle, hoping to capture a moment's glory in the Yellow Jersey, or catapult their team leader to the podium on the Champs-Élysées. Million-dollar contracts, global sponsors, mechanics, chefs and physicians attend to the riders' every need to ensure their peak performance, keeping the limbs supple and the state-of-the-art racing machines humming as they power, sprint and climb around the country every July.

The Race Across America is an altogether different prospect. At 3,000 miles coast to coast it is 50% longer than the Tour de France.

Critically, RAAM is not a stage race. The Tour is generally split into 20 or so stages. The stages start around lunchtime and can be anywhere from 100–200 miles in length, at the end of which the riders stop, have a shower, massage, eat, sleep and recover in a hotel until the next day. The Tour winner is the rider who, cumulatively, is quickest across the stages. In RAAM, when the gun fires at the start line in Oceanside, California, the clock is ticking until the finish line on the east coast. There are no breaks, no rest days. 'Stop' and you lose time. 'Sleep' and you fall behind. RAAM is an ultra-endurance event, a breed of sporting quest far beyond the ordinary. It is peerless in its length, difficulty and physical and mental intensity.

For this reason, it attracts a unique group of individuals who compete in the solo division. You won't find professional cycling teams at RAAM. There is no prize money, no global television coverage, no fame and fortune, merely a place amongst an exclusive cadre of gladiators who have traversed a continent. In just under 4 decades of the race, only 347 individuals have officially completed the crossing as solo racers within the required time limit.

More people summit Mount Everest annually. Wolfgang Fasching, who has achieved both feats has claimed that while Everest is more dangerous, RAAM is more difficult.

The Race Across America started out in 1982 with just four riders: John Marino, Michael Shermer, John Howard and the eventual winner, Lon Haldeman, who finished the race in an amazing 9 days and 20 hours. The next year there were 11 starters, including the first woman, and only six finishers. In most years about half the solo starters do not finish because of heat, exhaustion and various other physical and mindset problems.

The 2012 race boasted the biggest ever field in most of the divisions. There were 45 solo riders, with 28 finishers. Some experienced problems within the first 24 hours, their race over before it really started. I'm sure they will be back to have another go, armed with what they've learned from their previous experience. Those people are the real legends of RAAM. They have decided to test themselves, and when they fall short they get up, dust themselves down and have another go until they get it done.

The Race Across America requires solo riders to finish within 12 days for the open male division, aged up to 50, and 13 days for the men over 50 and women. If you don't finish within the cut-off times, you're not an official finisher. Since its inception in 1982, RAAM has become one of the most respected and longest-running endurance sports events in the world. It is seen as a pinnacle of athletic achievement, not only in cycling circles but in the greater sporting community as well. No wonder, then, that Outdoor magazine voted it the toughest race on the planet. After that first year, with its four pioneering participants, it quickly grew in popularity. It was covered by national television and the race captured the public's imagination. Teams were added in 1992 and quickly became the most popular and fastest-growing segment of the race.

It's been known to spit out some of the most experienced riders within their first 24 hours, riders with years of competition under their belt. This is definitely not a race for the faint of heart. If you have any doubts in your mind or if your ego is too big, the race will throw everything at you and break you – as I know well from my own first RAAM experience.

I didn't know about the Race Across America until 2004, when I asked my best mate to think about an event we could both do together following an injury I picked up racing one of my daughters up a set of stairs on holiday. I'd ripped my calf muscle and achilles and, as amusing as it was for my kids to see me hobbling around for the next ten days, it effectively ended my Ironman participation for a while.

Gary came up with the idea of competing in RAAM as a four-man team and it didn't take me long to say yes. After phone calls to a few more friends, we'd decided to put together an all-Ironman team to ride together in the 2005 race. We worked out we'd need to raise £30,000 to cover the costs of taking part, including flights, accommodation, support, transport and everything else involved in taking a team from the UK to America. To make it possible, we needed sponsorship and we all agreed we'd do our bit to try to raise the necessary funds.

We gave ourselves from July until December 2004 to see how we got on with finding the sponsorship required, especially as my three fellow riders were nervous about progressing if we didn't have a large chunk of the money backing us.

By December, I was the only one that had managed to get any sponsorship and all three of my teammates decided to pull out. This was a big shock for me as I was completely committed to being at the start line in June. Once I realised I wasn't going to talk any of them around, I got on with recruiting a new team. I knew enough people in the Ironman world and it didn't take too long before I had two more riders lined up: brothers Clive and Ian Middleton. Within a week we had our fourth rider, Stewart Wilson, and we were off training, while juggling our lives and looking to pull it all together. At the same time, we all agreed to look for three crew members each to support us.

I was the driving force behind the team, and before we knew it we were in San Diego, everyone squeezed into a motel with our RV and cars parked out in the back of the hotel car park. From memory, we even had a couple of the crew sleeping in the RV to save on the budget.

We had a crew of 12 and thought we were fairly well-organised, but within the first six hours of the race start we almost imploded. Myself and Clive were paired together and we were due to hand over to Ian and Stewart at the second time station, but on a downhill section Clive was going so fast that he was even overtaking cars and we lost sight of him. Clive is extremely competitive and, full of adrenaline at the race start, he wanted to show everyone just how good he was on a bike. With no sight of Clive, we got onto our teammates at the next time station and told them to keep an eye out for him. He had set off without lights and it was beginning to get dark.

At the time though, Ian was filled with fear when he realised that we had lost Clive, and as you can imagine, he was deeply concerned for his safety with no lights and those huge American 18-wheelers. It's hard to describe the stress, worry and anger we all felt as we searched for Clive. Fortunately, we finally found him – riding with a competitor from another team in front of the safety of their race car. A meeting was convened with race director Lon Haldeman to decide what to do. We had already lost four hours because of this incident and I thought we were going to be disqualified for time infringements. In the end we only received a 15-minute time penalty, plus a 15-minute cooling off period, before we were allowed to re-enter the race.

Emotions were flying high within the team and this was only the start of the race. If everyone wasn't on edge already, this put us all into a pressure cooker that was sure to boil over again.

It was only later that we found out that Clive had carried his bike across a section of desert that separated the road he should have been riding on from the main freeway. Clive had only realised that he was on a parallel road when he saw the flashing lights of other racers and their follow-cars across the way. The section of desert Clive went across with his bike was apparently filled with various unfriendly snakes and he was lucky he didn't get bitten.

Due to the stressful start everyone began to over-compensate, and by day two the planned sleep shifts had been missed and the crew started to fall apart. Small errors and tiny arguments began to magnify. By the time we got to Trinidad, Clive and Stewart in particular were feeling the strain, being upset about losing time to other teams that we had ridden hard to catch.

We riders were at least able to recover and sleep when we weren't on the bikes, but the crew were really feeling it. They were under intense pressure not to make any more mistakes. And, what usually happens when you put yourself under too much pressure?

It all came to a head over the lack of communication. We'd been having trouble getting signals on our mobiles, and when Clive and I were due to hand over to Ian and Stewart we found we couldn't get any reception. Clive and I had already put in a fairly long shift and had done some serious climbing. We were both looking forward to our break but we didn't know when it was going to come. Clive started to lose it and told me he wanted to blame two of our crew members, for the communication breakdown. As team captain he told me it was my job to tell them they were responsible and to sort it out. I didn't hold the same view and was in a better state to see the bigger picture: without a crew, I knew, we weren't going to finish this race.

We eventually found our other team after having to cycle for a further 40 miles beyond our original meeting point. We'd stopped at a petrol station and this was where Clive really lost it. He exploded and had a major go at Andy about all of the perceived mistakes he had made. Andy, at a serious height and weight disadvantage, gave as good as he got. It came perilously close to fists flying.

Clive had got everything he needed off his chest, but at a high cost. I was in tears at what had just happened and told Clive I wasn't going to pedal another stroke until he said sorry and resolved the situation he had created. Clive did to his credit eventually apologise, but a black cloud was now hanging over the team, and it would follow us until we encountered something even more shocking and upsetting further down the road.

Even though we managed to get some rest, Clive and I were still awash with emotion when we were told the dreadful news by race officials that one of our fellow competitors, Bob Breedlove, had been killed after colliding with a pickup truck. It still makes we cry if I think too much about that terrible day. I was still crying as I rode away from the RAAM offical, and I found myself getting angry with Clive for what had happened earlier.

Somehow the shocking news of Bob's death put everything into perspective for me, made all of our minor problems come into focus, and I reminded Clive that we all had families and that an accident like Bob's could have happened to any of us. Bob was a complete RAAM legend and had a massive positive impact on everyone he came in contact with. He is with me still and continues to be an inspiration. Bob Breedlove left a positive fingerprint on everyone he interacted with and he transformed people with his kindness.

Our team eventually slipped into a pattern where everyone was taking their sleep breaks on time, and the riders settled into the groove of riding as fast as we could to remain competitive and make up the time we'd lost on day one. We tweaked our riding patterns for the night rides especially, doing longer stints to reduce the lengthy handover times that we worked out were really slowing us down.

Clive and I still to this day believe that we did most of the climbing, although it's fair to say that Ian and Stewart also felt that they had done most of the climbing. We had bragging rights, as it's certainly true that we climbed the punishing Wolf Creek Pass and most of the Appalachians, although Ian and Stewart did chip in with some much-needed help towards the end of those beastly, steep climbs which at times would be between 10-20% gradient.

When we eventually crossed the finish line the feeling was more of relief than celebration. It felt as though there was no time to enjoy the moment. We were on a tight schedule, having the awards banquet to attend that evening and then the RV and support cars to clean and return, before packing our things to fly home the following day. We did as a team get to have a few beers at the banquet, and it was the first time we really got to appreciate what we'd achieved: fourth place overall with a time of 6 days and 15 hours.

Discounting the time we'd lost during the lengthy nighttime changeovers and the drama of the first day, we could have placed second.

To finish off the RAAM drama, we got completely lost getting from Atlantic City back to Newark airport. We were so late we had to ditch the RV in front of the airport departures building, leaving Stewart, who had a later flight, to deal with the traffic police. To cap it all, one of our drivers, who had been driving the RV, lost a wing mirror in our rush to get to the airport, so the repair bill for that, plus the airport parking fines, only added to our final costs for the race.

We were a rookie team and crew, that is true and there is no way you can finish this race without the incredible support of the crew who fixed things on the go and pushed through their own challenges with sleep deprivation and everything else the race throws at you. To be able to compete without some of the in-fighting that took place within the team of riders and crew was going to be something I wanted to experience. This was so I could test to see whether I would buckle under the physical and mental pressure of racing solo, so I sat on this for a year and then signed up for the 2007 race as a solo rider.

But despite everything, it had been an amazing experience and there were so many lessons learnt that we were able to apply to our own lives and future races.

Since that race some of the crew have gone back across America again with me and have remained in contact. Clive also went back in 2008, as part of a four-man team raising money and awareness for the CRY (Cardiac Risk in the Young) charity.

My birth mother & I before I was adopted

1st photo post my adoption with my new brothers Derek on the right & Jerry on the left

My Dad Peter Rees and the 3 boys they adopted in Alibon Park NSW Australia

My Mum Daisy Rees & I having fun in a photo booth 8 years old

Peter Rees old passport photo

Daisy Rees old passport photo

Our classic old caravan on holiday somewhere in NSW Australia 12 years old

My 1st triathlon in 1982 at Nepean NSW Australia, John Ross far left, me 2nd from the right

John Ross & I at the Nepean triathlon 1983, check out our new trisuits!

Gary Rogers & I at the Boxing day 10 mile run in 1984, UK

Me at the end of the 112 bike ride of the Hawaii Ironman in 1985

Me about 8 miles into the Hawaii Ironman marathon 1985

Me finishing the Hawaii Ironman in 1985 in 11 hours 22 mins

Gary Rogers and I happy with our Hawaii Ironman medals 1985

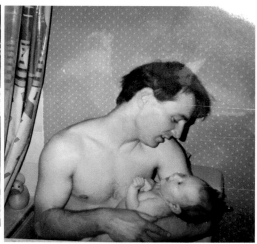

Me chilling the day after finishing the Hawaii Ironman 1985

My eldest daughter Megan & I 1990

Megan & I

My favourite photo of Megan as a toddler

Me with Megan & Elliot my eldest son in St Albans UK

Megan & I on holiday in Staithes Yorkshire UK

Sam my youngest son & I, again one of my favourite photo's of Sam

Daisy & I

Elliot & Daisy my youngest daughter on Bournemouth beach UK

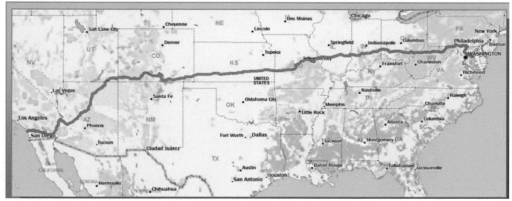

The Race Across America cycle route

The famous pier at Oceanside California

Finish photo of the 2005 4 man team. We finished 4th overall in 6 days 15 mins. Left to right Jim Rees, Clive Middleton, Ian Middleton, Stewart Wilson all Ironman Team

Me at the summit of Wolfe Creek Pass in 2005 Raam as part of the 4 man team

Enrico sporting our gilet with the built for greatness quote

The lucky coin given to me by a Raam enthusiast at the B&L bike shop before the start of 2007 race, my first solo Raam

Raam officials at the inspection in Betty's parking lot

Crew photo celebrating a successful inspection and race ready

Me just before the solo start of Raam 2007

John Evans my crew chief and Enrico Illuminati my doctor at the start

Paris Golden & Enrico Illuminati waiting at the start of the leap frog support

Entering the furnace which is the Mojave desert

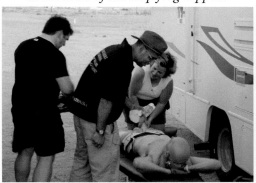

Just over 6 hours into the race and I suffered from stomach issues due to the heat and a dodgy chicken sandwich, this caused me to lose 4 hours off the bike and the race had only just started!

Ready to face my first night of Raam post my stomach issues

The following morning entering Arizona

Feeling wide awake on my way towards Yarnel Grade

This guy walked out of the Arizona desert to come and see why there was so much traffic

Climbing Yarnel Grade for the 1st time as a solo racer

The race car keeping me protected from the traffic as I focus on climbing

This Raam enthusiast had no idea his car was on fire in the short time it took him to jump out to take a photo of me as I cycled towards the turnoff point to Tuba City

Just turned right off the main downhill road from Flagstaff to Tuba City

The final climb to Tuba City

Cycling towards Kayenta

On my way towards the Rocky Mountains

At the top of Cuchara Pass

Wolfe Creek pass in the distance

Completely shattered and freezing at the top of the Wolfe Creek pass, just under 12,000 feet

Me passing Tom Seabourne who eventually pulled out later in the race, this was the other side of Wolfe Creek pass

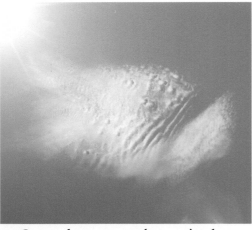

Crazy what you see when you're sleep deprived, for me this looked like a piranha

One of my favourite snacks, this was taken after Camdentown where the neck brace was fitted due to shemmer neck issues, a problem for some ultra cyclists

Cycling towards Marthasville

Eating off the bike which is a big no no!

A misty dewy morning in Missouri

Focused chasing the cut off time

Beautiful sunset

Patrick Autissier & I at the final time check both of us becoming 1st time Raam solo finishers

The makeshift awards held at a small pub in Atlantic City with the team

Tracey & Sam, which was an emotional reunion

I think Sam was trying to tell me something!

Sam said that he would come back and beat my time when he was older, me having a well deserved beer

Fabio & Nicoletta with their son Rocco at the official banquet in 2005

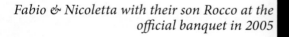

The RV, race ready in 2008

2008 solo start

Co-crew chiefs Donna & Mike keeping me cool before the race start, Nicola Pendleton giving me words of encouragement

Mike handing out a gel on the way to Flagstaff

The climb to Flagstaff

*Monument valley,
one of my favourite
parts of Raam*

*You can see that I'm happy
in this amazing part
of the race*

These trucks are big and fast

Off the bike for a quick break

Rick Boethling & I chatting on the other side of the Rocky Mountains

Problems with nose bleeds post the high altitude of the Rocky Mountains and me messing about pulling faces for the crew

The inspirational one arm cyclist Beny Furrer who I finally caught post climbing the Rockies, unfortunately Beny didn't finish that year

Somewhere in the middle of Raam

Between Jefferson &
Washington time stations,
Clive Middleton and his 4
man team went past me.
Lovely to be able to chat with
such a close friend who went
on to finish 2nd overall

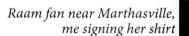

Raam fan near Marthasville,
me signing her shirt

Always nice to stop for Raam fans

Another stunning sunset

> *"Great spirits have always
> encountered violent opposition from
> mediocre minds."*
>
> ALBERT EINSTEIN

CHAPTER 4

Going Solo and Getting to the Start Line

Trying to remember when I made the decision to compete in RAAM as a solo rider is a little tricky. My first real thought of the solo riders was when I went to see them off at the start line in 2005.

Clive and I had ridden down to the start and I remember him telling me to check out the legs of the female cyclist in front of us. You can imagine Clive's shock when he rode up to have a chat with this rider and quickly realised that it was in fact the pony-tailed male rider Fabio Basiolo from Italy.

About five days later we passed Fabio somewhere in Kansas. I slowed down to have a chat with him and wished him well for a safe finish. The fresh face that had lots of Italian energy at the start had vanished and was replaced with the typical vacant stare that you see in all solo riders by that stage of the race. Fabio finished third and I got to spend a little more time with him at the awards banquet and meet his wife and newly-born son, Rocco.

I was also lucky enough to meet the Slovenian cyclist Jure Robic, who had won the solo race, and the second-place finisher and rookie of the year, Chris MacDonald. I was blown away by the fact that these guys had ridden every mile of the race alone, and we had just done it as part of a four-man team and were still shattered. Chris and Fabio were noticeably vacant, as they had only just finished and had arrived at the banquet with little or no rest.

I think this was when the seed was sown for me. I thought to myself what a test it would be to compete as a solo rider. Did I have what it took to finish this beast of a race? I remembered the extreme weather conditions and the sheer amount of climbing we did as a pair of riders within a four-man team. Now I was trying to stretch my mind to think how anyone could ride the whole race alone within the 12-day, 5-hour time limit. These guys looked more like gladiators than cyclists. They were bronzed and beaten up, and each had a glazed look in their eyes that told the story of what they had endured to make it to the finish line. I think it was that look I was searching for in myself. It triggered me to contemplate riding RAAM solo.

It must have been around April 2006 that I fully committed to the 2007 race. That was when I began searching for crew and support on how best to train for a 3,000-mile bike race. My first recruit was Donna von Tunk, my physiotherapist. She was born in Australia and I was lucky to have bumped into her in our local village back in 2001 when I was looking for a sports massage. We connected immediately, and until this day I haven't found anyone else who not only has the knowledge but also the know-how and touch that Donna has. She is also a chiropractor, which helped enormously as she was able to ensure my spine was properly aligned for the race.

The core part of my crew came together fairly quickly. Another close friend,

John Evans, didn't take long to consider my offer of the role of crew chief. He had a corporate background as a senior manager in a pharmaceutical company and prior to that had been a psychologist. John is also well-organised and calm under pressure.

I also asked Paris Golden, a buddy I met through my role as a coach and whose kind words introduced this book. We'd become close and our friendship had become a powerful bond. Paris had been through a tough phase personally, and was between jobs when I was recruiting for the race. The timing of getting Paris on board couldn't have been better and he was looking forward to the challenge of supporting me across America.

Another close friend was Enrico Illuminati from Milan. He was like a little brother to me. We'd met through a company we'd both worked for in 2000. When I later branched out and started my own company, Enrico and I stayed in touch and did some work together in Europe. Enrico was a doctor with a speciality in sports medicine and he had already supported a team in a couple of ultra-races. I felt his medical experience would be handy to have on board.

I was also able to recruit Steve Green, one of the stars of our 2005 four-man crew. Steve is the sort of guy you want around on a dark night if you come across any trouble. He has a heart that drives him to do his best in anything he takes on. Steve would smash through a wall if you needed him to and there was no job that was too big a stretch for him. If it needed doing he'd just do it and wouldn't wait for someone else to start. He'd just get stuck in.

John Evans also brought on board a friend of his called Rex, a training consultant whose approach was to take leadership groups out on a yacht and observe them as a team and then give them feedback on their performance.Unfortunately, Rex had an urgent client request and needed to pull out one week before we were due to fly over to the states. Paris was doing back flips, as for me I knew the nature or running your own business and was ok with the ebb and flow of the crew, I saw it more in terms of the movie Field of Dreams. I believed very strongly that the right people would ultimately show up and support me in my attempt to get from the West to the East coast of America safely and within the cut off time.

We managed to replace Rex as Steve convinced a close friend of his called Mike to join us. Mike was a perfect fit. He worked himself into the ground during the race, taking care of the RV with Steve. Salt of the earth, that man.

Our other crew member was nutritionist Judy Watson. She took care of the various extra vitamins and minerals I would need during the race and did all of my cooking, and kept me interested in eating and drinking throughout the race.

On top of our crew, I also contacted Karen Walsh, an ex-BBC documentary producer. I thought that she might be interested in filming our attempt at breaking the British record. Unfortunately, Karen was busy filming elsewhere but recommended a couple of other friends who might be interested. As it turned out, Richard Swift, a young film producer, stepped up and was really excited by the whole project. By the time we arrived in the USA, Richard had story-boarded what he was looking for and made all the pre-race shots he needed to ensure he had the correct footage to edit the film into an interesting story.

Little did we know what was to unfold in this epic journey across America.

Getting to the start line with a full complement of crew and with a rough plan of riding as much as possible, with power naps along the way, was about as much detail as we'd worked out.

We'd planned to be in the States for a week before the race began, to get ourselves ready and prepare the RV properly. This left me free to ride up and down the coast, following the pelicans, whilst the crew completed their logistical tasks. The pelicans reflected the laid-back Californian lifestyle along the coast, tanned surfers and people just getting on with their lives in what appeared to be a playground of fun in and around Oceanside.

On one of my first rides out along the coast I stopped at B&L Bike and Sports at Solana Beach and booked my bike in for a service for the following day. When I returned to the bike store, they told me the service would take about an hour. As I chatted to the staff about the race a customer came up to me and asked to shake my hand. He was almost overwhelmed as he had never met anyone who had competed in the race. I was quick to tell him that I hadn't finished the race yet as a solo rider. When my bike was finished, I paid up and left and found that the same customer was waiting for me, 45 minutes later, at the front of the shop. He kept telling me how lucky he was to have met me. So lucky, in fact, that he insisted on giving me his lucky St Michael coin, which bore the following inscription: "O St Michael, give us your strength to defeat our fears and to rise up to any challenge." I was flattered and I kept the coin in my back pocket for the whole of the race as I wove my way across America.

I didn't know then, but the timing of that gift was perfect, especially in the message it gave. It was only later I'd realise just how much I would need to dig deep into my soul to be able to finish what I had started.

Race Day 2007

The race started at 9:00am local time, or 12:00pm "RAAM time", seeing as the event is measured on Eastern seaboard time – some 3,000 miles away – to confuse our bodies further.

Then, coincidentally and to my surprise, the race officials read out "Our Deepest Fear" by Marianne Williamson, one of my favourite poems that I had posted on my bio, and it was read out by one of the officials just before the race got under way.

Filled with energy we cycled off to the staging post some 10 miles down the road where there would be a staggered start, with a two-minute gap between each rider. Although I had already met and spoken with the legend Jure Robic, what was about to unfold competing in RAAM became vividly clear when Jure rode past me fairly early on, in full race mode, down on his clip-on tri-bars. As he went past me, Jure wished me good luck and I shouted back for him to stay safe and wished him well.

The crew weren't on direct follow at this point in the race. They'd positioned themselves about 25 miles further on, before the climb to Palomar mountain in order to hand me some energy drinks. It was hot and it's a tough start to the race, going from sea level to just over 5,000 feet within the first 56 miles. I arrived at the first-time station and the race nerves had taken hold of me. I was barking orders at the crew, which is very unlike me, and I was given a couple of new bottles of drink, becoming annoyed that one of them was only a 500ml bottle and I was about to head out into the extreme heat of the Mojave desert. It was my first hissy fit of the race, but I quickly apologised for it further down the road.

I had decided that I was going to use a combination of energy drinks and solid foods for the race. Every rider has their own nutritional strategy, with some opting for a liquid-only diet, for example, but I felt that a blend would work best for me. Probably about 70 miles into the race I put in a request for a chicken wrap, one of my favourite snacks. The crew hadn't prepared any solid food for me, so they stopped at a roadside shack and purchased what was described as a chicken wrap and I gladly ate it. I'm still not sure whether it was the wrap or whether it was my body's reaction to the extreme heat of the desert, but I ended up having a major meltdown about 100 miles into the race.

I had to stop and have a lie down in the race car with the air conditioning on full blast. I'm not sure how long I stopped but I realised that I still wasn't OK when I got back on my bike and had to take an extended stop at Salt Lake for a good few hours. As I eased onto the massage couch I knew something was wrong. Waves of nausea were rippling through me, tickling my toes and then rising upwards to my middle and shocking my abdomen. The waxing and waning seduced me into thinking these cycles were only temporary maladies.

Perhaps a spot of indigestion? If I sit very still for a moment I'm sure it will pass, I told myself. But the frequency and amplitude of the organ grinding rapidly began to increase. I narrowed my stare and fixed it on a rock on the ground. I sensed my support crew looking on, concerned. Just 200 miles into a 3,000-mile race and I was sitting on my backside desperately attempting to retain my dignity while my competitors surged ahead. Dignity quickly became a non-priority. "I'm going to be sick," I slurred to my helpers.

They scurried around and hoisted me into the motorhome and to the toilet – a plastic cubicle barely large enough to sit down in. With my feet out of the door I knelt at the polycarbonate altar and took ease of my day's consumption. It was a heady cocktail of sports drinks, protein replacement mixtures, energy gels and that bloody wrap – all now making their way into the motorhome's waste tank.

The morning of the race start I had been giddy with excitement, waking early through a mixture of jetlag and anticipation. The Race Across America had consumed me for the past three years and here I was about to start – as a rookie solo rider. I had devoted most of my waking hours and dreaming state to this race. I was operating out of awareness and created a blind spot and I had sacrificed time with my family in order to train. I'd turned away work, got into debt and brought financial stress upon my family. I had been single-minded in my obsession and vision for competing in the world's toughest endurance race. It was like waking up on Christmas morning and finding all the toys you could ever imagine spread in front of you (including two bikes). I was about to live my dream. But it was turning into a bit of a nightmare now, as illness took hold of me.

That's how I felt as I emerged gingerly from the support vehicle. Purged, I felt relieved but exhausted. I had ridden for the last seven hours in the searing heat and none of my training in the UK had prepared me for the furnace-like conditions of the Mojave desert. After an initial climb of a few thousand feet, the course descends to below sea level and into a radiating red dustbowl. No shade, no breeze, no protection, no relief. The hot, dry air parched my mouth and throat. It was like breathing air from a hair dryer, I felt as though I was being dehydrated from the inside out, internally combusting.

I re-started just as it was getting dark, in last place. So, I clipped in my pedals and started my first night of riding. I felt a lot better by now, but I do want to say to other riders: beware of any food that your crew haven't prepared themselves, getting a snack from a takeaway store, could result in time lost off the bike.

Even though I'd had a really debilitating purge, my energy levels were really good through the night and I was really excited that all was now going smoothly. The course that evening took in the interstates, the equivalent of the British motorways, adding more danger as trucks flew by at 70 mph.

The following morning, we were greeted with the first of many spectacular sunrises as we headed into the Arizona deserts and towards time station seven. This is where we had our first encounter with some of the many interesting people you meet as you travel across this huge landscape.

The time station crew had organised a small paddling pool full of ice-cold water for riders and their crew to have a little soak and I was delighted to get some time off the bike before I climbed Yarnell Grade. After my previous day's indisposition, I met what looked like an old miner who had just wandered out of the desert. He had an impressive grey beard that must have been at least a foot long and was in awe of the fact that people were cycling across America within 12 days. He thought that you'd have to be nuts to do such a thing and said that it used to take travellers months to go across the continent in the old days. I sometimes think this old prospector might have been my first hallucination of the race, but we caught him on camera so I guess he was real!

I climbed Yarnell Grade in the heat of the afternoon and I then climbed through Scull Valley just before it started getting dark. This is where I saw my first live snake, a black and white diamond head rattlesnake lying on the side of the road soaking up the last bit of heat from the day. He scared the hell out of me, but I was moving fast enough to not let him get at me. Even though I grew up in Australia and had seen a few snakes in my time, I still don't like them that much. They give me the shivers.

I then had an ascent of 8,000 ft, up Mount Francis as night fell. On the other side of the mountain we joined Route 66 and the interstate. Sleep deprivation from four hours rest in the last 36 hours was heaping further challenges on me as I negotiated the busy road. I arrived safely, but exhausted, in Flagstaff and took my first big sleep of the race as the sun began to rise. I woke having spent a few hours asleep in the RV and ready to head towards Tuba City and the Painted Desert. It was mid-morning and I was starting to catch some of the other riders.

On the main road towards Tuba City, we drove past a RAAM fan who had parked their car on the side of the road to take some photos. As I passed by I saw flames coming out of the front of his red Dodge Duke. The poor chap hadn't realised the danger of parking in the long, dry grass at the side of the road. I arranged for our crew to turn around and take him to the next service station, but his car was a wreck by then, burnt out beyond repair.

The rock formations of the desert were just remarkable and I was grateful that I was able to see this part of America and I felt a deep connection with the native American Indians as we entered the Navajo Nation. I'm not sure why there was this deep connection, maybe it was that I had read *Bury My Heart At Wounded Knee* by Dee Brown – this extraordinary book tells how the American Indians lost their land, lives and liberty to white settlers pushing westward. Woven into an engrossing saga of cruelty, treachery and violence are the fascinating stories of such legendary figures as Sitting Bull, Cochise, Crazy Horse and Geronimo.

Or it could have been that as a young boy growing up, I was fascinated with cowboys and indians and watched my share of all of the old spaghetti westerns and now I was about to cycle through the Navajo Nation.

I think there was also the fact that I had grown up in Australia where the native population of the Aborigines were also subjected to similar treatment from the white man!

And, possibly at a deeper level I was going through struggles of my own that I could relate to and connect with not just during the race but within my life in general.

With temperatures rising and the threat of twisters ever present, I arrived mid-afternoon at the next stop and took a precious rest period. I was back in the saddle by the evening, ascending 7,000 ft to Kayenta where the vista is dominated by the awesome Monument Valley, then we crossed the state line into Utah.

In darkness, I approached the famous Monument Valley peaks, including Mexican Hat. In the pitch black, myself and the crew were unable to appreciate the "Eighth Wonder of the World". My focus by then was to up the pace in order to reach the city of Cortez, Colorado, before the first cut-off point – the time at which each rider must have reached a designated position or be disqualified from the race. Having had two tough days in the desert, and with little rest, I needed to put in a phenomenal effort to attack the mountains of Utah and regain time to comfortably reach Cortez in time, which I did. I also began to overtake other riders as I grew stronger through each time station.

Then, as day three turned into day four, I now faced the prospect of the highest ascent of the race: 12,000 feet through Wolf Creek Pass in the Rocky Mountains.

As I rode higher into the mountains, conditions turned against the riders with temperatures dropping significantly at night. Many of the solo competitors began their ascent as night fell, myself included, and I faced the incredible challenge of severe climbs in the cold and dark. By this stage, all the riders were suffering from sleep deprivation. Some fell by the wayside, but I battled onwards, albeit slowly, and edged my way along the mountain pass. I was desperate to sleep and begged the crew to allow me to rest before I climbed Wolf Creek Pass, but they felt that it would be better if I continued onward and upward. I finally got to the top by being shouted at by Donna leaning out of the passenger-side window of the support car. There was even one occasion when Donna reached out and pulled me back from cycling over the roadside barrier as I was falling asleep in the saddle.

It was so cold that Donna didn't stay hanging out of the window for very long and she retreated to the warmth of the car, with John using the car horn each time they saw my shoulders slump with sleep. I jumped out of my skin each time he did it, but it worked and I stayed awake. When I arrived at the top of Wolf Creek, both John and Donna gave me a big hug and I just broke down and cried, I was so exhausted and frozen.

After a quick 15-minute power nap I was mustered by both of them and set off to descend the mountain. Just a couple of minutes in, though, I was so completely frozen that I had to stop and cover both of my feet with a rubbish bag and put a bin liner over my cycling kit in an attempt to stay warm. I arrived at the next time station exhausted and emotional, but still filled with the dogged determination that had delivered me this far.

After the stresses of Wolf Creek the crew were unsure of how I would respond to the next stages, which built to another severe climb from 6,000 to 9,000 ft. The first stage was relatively flat, allowing me to gather myself for the ascents to come. Keeping a steady pace through the second stage on the gradual ascent of La Veta Pass was measured riding, culminating in the final stage – Cuchara Pass and another 3,000 ft climb.

I remember late in the afternoon, as I was riding through the valley, there was a farm on the right-hand side of the road and all of a sudden a dog came out of nowhere and ran straight at me. He was huge. A demon dog! I upped my pace, but he was determined to take a chunk out of my tanned leg. I couldn't shake him off, and by now the crew were becoming increasingly stressed. Donna leaned out of the follow-car and gave an almighty roar. It worked. The dog turned tail and ran back to the house, yelping.

At the age of 5 or just turning 6, I was bitten by the dog next door: it was a mongrel, a cross between dingo and wolf and was chained up and used as a guard dog. I was playing with my toy cars with the neighbour's kid and went to grab one of my cars that had ended up near the dog. I looked him in the eye and thought I'd be OK to retrieve my car, but I guess my nerves and quick movement caused him to lash out in the only way he knew! It all happened so quickly and I ended up at the local doctor's surgery getting five stitches to sow my upper lip back on. The stitches hurt like crazy but it was the tetanus injection that worried me, as a young kid my imagination took over and I thought that the needle was going to come out of the top of my head!

So, I guess you can see why that incident spiked my adrenaline, and the combination of the breathtaking scenery and clear mountain air boosted my energy. The support crew enjoyed one of the prettiest stages and I had a great performance in the bag before nightfall.

I've never been camera-shy and I was photographed and interviewed by the RAAM media team as we coasted into Trinidad ahead of schedule. As we did, thoughts of Bob Breedlove came flooding back to me from the 2005 race.

Race Day Six

This was where the mountain passes and high peaks began to give way to rolling foothills and, eventually, high plains. Leaving Colorado, we passed into Kansas and America's bread basket. It was an endless flat vista of crop and beef production, punctuated by enormous concrete grain silos.

In contrast to the mountain climbs, the flatlands of Kansas should have been a welcome relief, were it not for an energy-sapping headwind that soon began to take its toll on my neck. It's a common problem amongst ultra-cyclists, where the neck muscles are so fatigued that the rider is unable to keep his head up. It's known as Shermer Neck, named after the ultra-cyclist Michael Shermer, who was the first to experience the phenomenon. It prevents you from looking forward from the prone aero position – the most efficient cycling style. This was now another issue to contend with, but I pushed on and upped the effort to drive forward through the wind and pain.

However, a dramatic night in Kansas was soon to unfold. Pushing through to the night shift the effort of the day's riding began to catch up with me and my pace slowed as I valiantly cycled onwards. Darkness brought on an overwhelming need for sleep and I was allowed to take an hour's rest in the support car. Six days and 1,300 miles of cycling had caught up with me and my tiredness rapidly turned to sickness. After an hour of slow progress, it was clear that I was completely out of energy. The crew decided to take me off the course and find a motel room for a few hours' rest. By now I was struggling to eat enough calories and was getting sick of the taste of the various sports' drinks I was using to keep me fuelled. Judy was doing her best, providing a selection of high-calorie snacks, but it was still a struggle.

We headed north in the car to Dodge City, the only significant conurbation nearby. It was 1:00 am and the crew, having had to coax me along through a difficult few hours, were feeling the strain too. Eventually, we found a motel. Paris was driving, and in an effort to get as close to the motel's entrance as possible – I was so tired I could barely walk from the car to the foyer – he pulled up under an awning overhanging the way in. But he had forgotten that my spare bike was still up on the roof rack. My heart sank as I heard the sickening and unmistakable crunch of the handlebars being mangled as the roof rack was torn off.

Paris almost broke down in tears when he realised what had just happened. He looked at me, ready for a right talking to. Yet, even after everything I'd already had to contend with that evening, my instant response was: "I never liked that bike much anyway – it was giving my neck gip." Paris couldn't believe I was so relaxed about a pair of ruined handlebars that had cost £500. Truth was, my neck problems were so bad I wouldn't have been able to ride that bike again anyway. It was my time trial bike and it was set up in such a way that my neck would probably have snapped if I'd tried.

While I grabbed a few hours' sleep, Steve and Paris utilised their best handyman skills with a roll of duct tape to repair the roof rack. We then drove back to where we'd left the course the night before and I completed the remaining 17 miles of the section to Montezuma. I was certainly pleased that stage had come to an end.

Race Day Seven

One week into the race, we were making further progress along the endless plains of Kansas. After the outskirts of Witchita I comfortably reached the second cut-off target of the El Dorado time station. I was then able to enjoy a well-earned rest and a fresh chicken salad!

Heading off that evening, it was clear that my neck wasn't getting any better. The crew attempted to relieve the pain and discomfort by fitting me with a neck strap, which gave some support but was not an effective solution. Neither were any of the other improvisations we tried. Then, after meeting former RAAM winner and Shermer Neck sufferer Alan Larson at the Fort Scott time station, the crew developed an idea based on constructing a brace to hold my chin up. But that would have to wait until the morning, and in the meantime I still had to ride through the pain. Finally, at around 2:00am, the pain was pretty unbearable as we stopped at a roadside garage while the crew rigged up a makeshift neck support by taping a Pringles tube to my handlebars so that my chin could rest on it. It worked – for about two minutes until I went over a bump in the road and almost broke my jaw.

I just had to accept that I was going to have to ride on with my failing neck. I could just about hold my head up for about 30 seconds before my neck muscles collapsed, forcing my head to droop. Then, I'd force my head back up, and the whole painful process would begin again. It was crazy, yet I was determined not to let it stop me from finishing the race. I was all in. Nothing was going to get in my way. It was a bit like not taking a no from a possible customer, I just continued to persist and not give up!

The constant headwind I'd endured cycling across Kansas had forced me to eat a good portion of humble pie. Here I was, attempting to set a new British record, and I literally couldn't hold my head up. But by now the record wasn't what the race was about for me. It had become a quest to finish what I had started, a test of my inner strength. An attempt to see if I really did have what it took to complete this brutal race within the cut-off time.

Race Day Eight

We left Kansas, and I was happy to see the back of the place after all the trials and tribulations it had brought. We entered Missouri, encountering a landscape of rolling green hills that reminded me of the UK. Suddenly everything felt more welcoming, familiar and comfortable.

Then, as living embodiment of that, as I cycled in blistering heat towards time station 32, a young girl of about six appeared, standing outside her house along the roadside. She was holding ice lollies and a jug of cold water, which she offered to me. Her parents were RAAM fans and found out I'd been having neck issues, and they wanted to show their support. That child was like a little angel and I was blown away by her small – but also huge – act of kindness.

My neck problem was becoming increasingly serious and, based on Alan Larson's advice, Steve and Paris somehow constructed a chin and neck brace from some one-inch PVC piping, a belt, and an NFL football helmet chin strap. It didn't look too pretty, but it did the trick. In fact, I wore it for the rest of the race.

Paris was so impressed with his invention I think he considered registering a patent. This Bulldog spirit, make-do-and-mend endeavour caused a media frenzy in Camdenton where we were stationed. It even attracted the attention of the local paper, the Sun Leader, as well as the RAAM media team. I could imagine the headline: "Mad Brits in Neck Brace Shocker!". Unfortunately, we didn't hang around long enough to see the final article. I had a race to ride!

With the neck brace in place I set off on the next leg, bound for Jefferson City, an unremarkable place, except for the replica of the White House, where we found a lonely, unmanned time station. Then it was on through the night to Marthasville following the Missouri River. This was a long, flat section punctuated by two significant ranges of hills, both of which I tackled during the witching hours. On one of the descents, as I flew downhill, I actually fell asleep for a split second. It's a sensation that's very hard to describe, a little like the feeling you have when you are dreaming of falling and you wake up with a start. To my horror, this is exactly what happened to me as I careered off the road and down the side of a very steep gravelly hill. Somehow, I kept control of the bike and managed to get back on the road without crashing. After the adrenaline rush from this incident had worn off, the rest of the stage turned into a long, tiring session through the night. There are so many moments during the race up til this point where I had feelings of being invincible and at other points where I felt like a drunk on a bike; during the early hours between 2am - 5am I was feeling like I had been drinking all night and needed my bed.

I had slowed significantly in the hours before dawn, and had slept less than one hour in the previous 24. But as the sun rose so did my speed. Critically, this had to be maintained if I was going to meet the next cut-off point in Indianapolis at 11:00am that morning. By then, I would be just over 2,200 miles into the race.

This is where I started to feel a bit more pressure being applied by the crew, I was being managed really tightly regarding my sleep breaks and any time I was having off the bike. The truth is that it's really important for the crew to be all over their rider wanting time off the bike, so the tug of war between me wanting a break and the crew wanting me to keep moving forward started at this point in the race.

I would end up behaving a bit childish at some points and having a mini hissy fit if I wasn't allowed a 30-minute power nap but would happily submit if I got 15 minutes as they drove a hard bargain when managing a guy who at these times appeared to be 3 times over the alcohol limit on a bike!

Race Day Nine

Crossing from Missouri to Illinois the terrain altered little, being mostly flat or gently rolling hills through farmland and small-town America. As I rode through this landscape it soon became apparent something was not quite right with my food and drink intake.

I was starting to retain water at a dangerous rate and I was beginning to bloat alarmingly. At one point I stopped for a 10-minute rest and had to get one of the crew to cut me out of my expensive cycling shorts and top to relieve the pressure. I looked as though I'd been on a diet of fish and chips for weeks, rather than competing in an elite sports cycling race. The discomfort was having a big impact on my performance. My face was swollen and pudgy, as though I'd just gone 10 rounds with a heavyweight boxer – and lost, badly. My hands and feet were swollen, too, and I developed painful heat spots on the balls of my feet that got worse the longer I rode. We discovered that I was getting the salt and potassium balance wrong in my nutrition intake. It was something else that needed to be fixed.

Somehow, though, I managed to make good progress and reached the next cutoff point in Indianapolis with two hours to spare. In fact, at this stage the opportunity to break the British record was still within reach. I was riding in a pack with three other racers, and that helped us to drive each other on. My three amigos were John Spergeon, who was attempting the race on a single speed bike with no gears (he had to change wheels for the uphill sections!), lanky Canadian Larry Optis, and the Frenchman Patrick Autissier.

As I started to leave Indianapolis behind, it started to rain and then just kept on raining for the next few hours. I remember the chin strap of my neck brace at this point was starting to cut just under my chin; the constant rain allowed a saw-like movement of the strap and this was another thing on a list of things I had to manage.

At that point the rain seemed to soothe the burning sensation I was getting from the open saddle sores on each side of my butt and even though that was one thing that was a small relief, I had started to develop an issue with my left knee which felt like a bit of bone was rubbing against another bit of bone!

All these issues can happen at once as they were with me at that point and sometimes they're easy to manage. Each of them I would typically rate in terms of pain on a scale of 1-10, with 10 being unbearable and 1 being barely noticeable. So at that point, my chin and knee were about a 6 each and my butt had gone from a gnarly 7 down to a very manageable 4.

This is where I used some of the tools I learnt through coaching that allowed me to manage my state and keep riding my bike. I imagined the pain and where it was in my body and visualised it moving down through my body to either my left or right foot depending on which side the pain was and then I imagined it exiting my foot.

Did it work? It certainly took my focus away from the pain I was feeling in that part of my body in that moment, so yeah I'd say it helped for sure.

Getting to Illinois was also a reminder that we'd reached the landmark of 2,000 miles down with 1,000 to go. I tentatively began to think about the end of the race, the finish line, and a comfortable bed to sleep in.

I was getting excited to see my wife, Tracey, along with her youngest daughter and our son Sam, as well as Tracey's mum who had all flown over. The plan was for Tracey to drive out to meet me toward the end of the race and become part of the crew for the final run into Atlantic City, then we'd catch up with the others after a couple of days.

Race Day Ten

Now riding constantly throughout the day and night, the concept of distinct days no longer had any meaning. I was either on the bike, eating or sleeping. The crew worked in shifts around me and so their patterns followed mine, snatching a nap or bite to eat whenever the opportunity arose.

The impact on me was obvious and unpredictable: sudden switches from alert and awake to nodding off; dramatic drops in speed, so that the steady line and rhythm of a strong rider turned into the uncertain wobble of a child just off stabilisers. For the following crew, their role became one of watching out for my sudden changes of speed and stability, and to coach and coax me along, feed me snacks and promise me treats. Whatever it took to keep me upright and moving forwards. The conditions took their toll on the crew, too. Tired and disoriented, they struggled to perform even simple mental arithmetic in order to work out bike speed averages and distance targets. Driving relatively slowly down long, straight roads, especially at night, is not exactly mentally stimulating. It's not unusual for a crew member to fall asleep at the wheel of the follow-car and hit their own rider. Thank goodness that didn't happen to me.

Crossing to Ohio I encountered more farming country. Small towns dotted the roadside: wooden houses painted white and pastel blue, rocking chairs on the verandas, and many, many expressions of patriotism decorating the front gardens and porches. The ubiquitous Star-Spangled Banner.

As the countryside became greener and more rolling I experienced a lot of rain in the form of a torrential downpour near Circleville. For me this was an annoyance rather than a drama. The rain was warm and I had wet weather gear. For the crew, having to get in and out of the car for my toilet breaks, kit changes and bike checks was less pleasant as their already too-long-worn clothes were now damp, steamy and a little stinky.

It's funny to write this but I had obviously developed that stare that all solo riders have long before this stage of the race. It's a little hard to describe apart from it being like you're in a state of shock and I think that's a fair way to think about it; your body is constantly sending signals to your brain to say stop and sleep. In a zombie-like state I just kept riding, holding on to the hope of seeing Tracey and the kids along with a warm hotel room and bath.

Race Day Eleven

Approaching West Virginia, the hills became more frequent and higher. As I crossed the border from Ohio the route took us from comfortable country roads onto the US 50E, a six-lane highway. The clear blue skies and strong sunlight reflecting off the white concrete sapped my energy. The roar of cars and trucks at 70 mph made communication virtually impossible and I was in effect isolated from the support vehicle. It was the busiest highway I had encountered since leaving California.

Having ridden through the night I was short of sleep and energy and the typical metronomic rhythm of my cycling began to stutter. The poor condition of the hard shoulder made the surface challenging, so I sought a better line in the slow lane. As I crossed the white line, I lost control of the bike and swerved across the carriageway. I had hit a gap in the concrete join and it diverted me straight across the motorway into the path of what looked like the 18-wheeler from the movie Dual hurtling at a ferocious speed straight at me. I literally cried out "Yikes" and bunny-hopped 180 degrees and scurried back to the right side of the road. I avoided catastrophe, but it was a reminder of the dangers involved in the race.

Traffic bearing down on you at frightening speeds, horns blaring, stones and debris being thrown all around; it was no place for the faint-hearted.

Clearly shaken, the crew guided me off the course at the first opportunity. Up a small country lane, we found a tree to sleep under and took some time out to restore our energy and courage. It was an event like this that had the potential to completely scare the shit out of anyone and it did rattle me more than just a bit but almost like Arnie from the Terminator movies I had made a commitment to just keep going, no matter what.

Continuing onwards, the 50E became quieter and, being a main route, provided a good surface for swifter progress. I was now in the foothills of the Appalachian Mountains, the last major range before the descent down to the east coast and Atlantic City. I had cycled 2,500 miles and was still on track to break the British record for the race. Having spent so much energy already, and the gruelling regime affecting my neck and swollen legs, I hoped I would have enough in the tank to climb the steep ascents of the Appalachians. The crew had seen two sides of my encounters with the mountains of Colorado: misery and despair at Wolf Creek, euphoria and triumph at Cuchara Pass. What would it be this time?

Race Day Twelve

Ascending the first peak in the early hours, I knew I would have to cover the Appalachians – a major American mountain range – in just one day in order to remain on track. I had always responded magnificently to these challenges in the past and I set about the climbs with grit and determination.

Completing the first mountain stage strongly, I was then struck down with a wave of tiredness. Sleep deprivation took hold and I could not escape its grip. I became irritable, making more and more sudden stops to pee or change kit, all taking precious time. Eventually, the crew allowed me to sleep in the car. But the unscheduled stops had blown the schedule for the British record. Of more concern was the fact that I was also in danger of falling behind the timetable to meet the cut-off to be an official RAAM finisher. I had to be in Atlantic City by 5:00pm on Friday. Failure to do so would mean I would not record a time and would be classed DNF – Did Not Finish.

The crew decided it was time to unlock the immense power in my mind to take me to the finish. Physically, I was in good shape and had good speed on the bike. The challenge was to draw on my inner strength to keep me in the saddle and pedalling.

Enrico woke me and presented me with a map of the USA, pointing out where I had started in Oceanside and then showing our current position. I had covered 90% of the route. Time to get back on the bike, he was saying. And that's what I did and resumed the climb.

Enrico was driving and Paris's navigation thus far had been impeccable, but with the end of Stage 49 in sight we came upon an intersection with Interstate 68. Confusing road signs, ambiguity in the route book and Paris's exhaustion resulted in us taking a wrong turn up the Interstate slip road. Having had the incident earlier on the 50E, the last place I needed to be was on one of America's major routes. Taking evasive action, Paris stopped me, picked up my bike and walked with me back down the slip road to the correct junction. Whether it was lost in translation I'm not sure, but Paris asked Enrico to carry along the interstate and come off at the next junction and meet us.

But, like in a scene from the movie, The Italian Job, Paris and I were passed by Enrico reversing at 20 mph back down the slip road, much to the bemusement of oncoming traffic. Clearly, living in Milan makes you a far braver driver than those of us from the home counties in the UK.

The next section to Hancock, Maryland, consisted of four major climbs which I completed in an aggressive time. I now embarked on the last two stages in the Appalachians, with three relatively simple climbs to go before the course descended to the Atlantic coast. I completed the first of these stages on schedule. We started the second section with a 1,000 ft climb, but as I reached the summit the sleep demon returned to haunt me. My schedule allowed no further breaks. In order to reach Atlantic City and complete the race before the cut-off, I would have to cycle almost continually. There were 217 miles to go and just 19 hours left.

Paris and Enrico pushed me onwards through the second climb but I was losing time. I wasn't going fast enough and was pleading with Paris to stop. I tried every tactic: humour, aggression, negotiation. I was cycling at 4-5 mph and swerving all over the place, a danger to myself and other road users. I knew my performance was deteriorating rapidly but also that to stop would throw away the possibility of a finish. Yet it was clear too that continuing at this rate was impossible. I stopped for a 15-minute break and snatched a nap. I then set off again, but after only a few miles my bike control failed and I was forced to stop again, this time for 30 minutes. I was right on the edge where I knew I was a danger to myself and yet I was still attempting to push those pedals to get to a destination that I had never been to before, the finish line of the Race Across America as a solo rider.

After 12 days of hard cycling through deserts, mountains, headwinds and searing heat, I had reached the point where sleep deprivation now ruled my physical and mental systems. The crew had pushed me on but I could no longer follow the instructions they were giving me. I was hallucinating, veering from one side of the road to the other.

Paris and Enrico decided it was time to bring the race to an end.

Their thoughts turned to me, Tracey and our children. The team's primary aim from the start had been to complete the race safely. With this in mind, the decision to stop was an easy one. I knew the consequences would be difficult to accept – all the preparation, effort and commitment from everyone involved meant that not achieving the end goal would be a massive and potentially destructive disappointment. From Paris and Enrico's point of view, they saw that their friend was in a very dangerous situation and were in the privileged position to remove that danger from me. They pulled over to the side of the road and prepared a bed in the back of the MPV for me to sleep in. Crew doctor Enrico recommended at least two hours' sleep and I was so depleted that I fell fast asleep instantaneously.

In terms of the race, they accepted that I would not finish inside the cut-off time.

I now had 190 miles to go to the finish line, and just under 13 hours left. That meant I would have to ride on at an average of 15 mph. My average speed to date had been between 10-12 mph. Only the winners of RAAM sustain averages of over 15 mph.

When they woke me at 4:20am, my first question was about the race: "So, where are we now?"

"I'm sorry Jim, you aren't going to finish within the cut-off time," Paris told me.

The look on my face was one of surprise and shock.

Paris tried to reassure me: "We will support you and finish the course with you. You will have cycled across America," was what he said.

I don't know where it came from, but I told Paris: "I know you did what you had to do, but nothing is impossible. I'm getting on the bike."

With that, I rubbed my head and slapped my face. Paris readied the bike and I set off at a terrific rate, back onto a steady line and consistent rhythm. Paris and Enrico felt sorry for me. They did not believe what I intended to do was possible. They were worried that I would blow up again and would be unable to cycle at all, or that I would limp on to the time station and my race would fall apart in front of me.

Even though I wasn't physically or mentally able to do complex mathematical equations at that point, I decided that I could cover the remaining miles in the time I had left. In the route book, the rest of the ride profile looked relatively flat. There were a number of climbs which usually wouldn't have been an issue, but given the speed I needed to maintain and the fact that I was shattered from cycling in a neck brace for just over 1,700 miles, it wasn't going to be easy.

I did not slow down and I covered the 12 miles to the next time station swiftly.

Paris and Enrico handed over to the other support crew of Tony, John and Donna for the next two stages. They were all a little bemused as I arrived, stripped off down to just my racing suit and announced: "Let's go, I'm going to do this."

I was stunned that the crew didn't believe that I could finish within the cut-off time and I was disappointed by their lack of faith. But this only spurred me on further to prove them wrong. I was going to use every ounce of energy I had to see this through, for my family, my crew, the sponsors and for my own self-esteem and self-confidence. I had to finish what I'd started.

Even though it was always obvious that this race was against the clock from the start, I now found myself under even more pressure. In my own head with 160 miles to go and 10 hours before the cut-off time, I realised I needed to average 16 mph. My mental state was solid and I knew that an average speed of 16 mph was easy in normal circumstances, but this was far from normal. I had cycled 2,880 miles and more than half of that was with the new addition of my neck support which, even though I had fully accepted I couldn't finish without it, was extremely uncomfortable. Throw in all of the sleep deprivation and the long list of hallucinations, physical fatigue and a body that was scorched by the blistering sun, I still had an unshakeable belief that I could get this done. Where did that belief come from? I believe it was from growing up in Australia where in general they have a positive mindset – I was always a sporty little kid that was fiercely competitive and I still am now. I really think competitive sports as a kid growing up instilled a truckload of grit in me and I've always attempted to instill that in my kids as they grew up. I would never let any of the kids beat me in a running race or anything competitive. The reason for that was that I believed that if they did eventually beat me, it was a real victory as they knew I'd never throw a race and this was my chance to show my kids what I stood for, that I wasn't going to quit and I was going to use every ounce of energy to finish this race.

I didn't really have to think about whether I could finish in time or not because my belief in myself was never in doubt in my head, I just needed to turn the pedals over faster than I had for most of the race – for goodness sake it was only 160 miles to go.

The course now moved into the beautiful fertile lands of Pennsylvania where Amish communities sit side by side with modern farms. The contrast is stunning, yet they seem to coexist happily together, neither seeming out of place.

Paris in our other vehicle was keeping watch on my progress and times. He saw that I wasn't slowing down. I was getting faster. Paris began to think: 'Surely this can't be done, can it?' Paris arrived at the final time station and waited for me and the crew to arrive. Although I had made rapid progress so far, Paris was concerned that I would not be able to sustain such a searing pace. I was also now in a city with cars, traffic lights and roadworks to contend with, all of which would slow me down.

The crew only started to believe at the final time station that maybe I did have a chance, albeit a very, very slim one, of finishing within the cut-off time. I arrived at the final time station needing to cover 60 miles in just under four hours.

The support crews swapped over and I set off again. After just 50 yards I had to stop. Puncture! My first of the race and right when I didn't need it. A quick wheel change sorted that, and I was back on course.

As we progressed the course began to change in our favour: long roads, less traffic and precious side and tailwinds. This helped me to keep the bike speeds at over 20 mph and race in the "aero" position – crouching down on the handlebars to minimise drag. The clock ticked on and the miles were consumed. Enrico drove in a typically aggressive Italian style to plough through the traffic, while Donna bellowed instructions and encouragement. Paris was navigating, his hands clenched vice-like to the route book. He now thought that I could do it, but that it was going to be very tight.

As I cleared the final time station I was cheered through by the rest of the crew. There were nine miles left to go. But then there was a jolt and a strange noise from the follow-car. It had driven over a bolt which was now embedded in the tyre. It was touch and go that the tyre would deflate. If it did I would have to go on alone and navigate my own way to the finish. I hoped that the tyre would hold out.

Still focused on finishing the race, I stopped myself from thinking about celebrations or victories. The 3,040 miles I had completed were filled with emotions and challenges. And here I was, just a few miles from the finish. Nothing was going to stop me now.

When I did in fact cross the finish line Paris and Enrico jumped from the car to embrace me. Paris told me what he witnessed that day was incredible, if not magical. My determination and belief drove me through my exhaustion and sleep deprivation to the point where I was able to extract an extraordinary performance and cycle quicker than I had at any point in the entire race.

I finished the race eight minutes inside the cut-off time. Richard Swift was there with his film camera and he got his story, which was shown as part of a No Limits series later that year on ITV – you can watch it via Youtube just type in the search Jim Rees Race Across America.

The race officials staged a makeshift award ceremony at a hotel just off the Board Walk of Atlantic City which is where the race finished that year. I was reunited with Tracey and her daughter and Sam along with Tracey's mum and I was full of emotion, I looked like Kurt Douglas from the movie Spartacus, all sunburnt and completely knackered! Sam had only just turned six and he was talking about breaking my record when he was older! He also took great delight in reminding me just how stinky I smelt, due to the time pressure of finishing within the cut-off time, I didn't have the luxury of changing into a clean kit or to wash before the race finished.

With the ceremony done, it was time to spend time with my beautiful woman and her youngest daughter and our son Sam, all 4 of us squashed into a motel room at the end of the night and I slept like a well-behaved newborn baby!

> *"Our greatest glory is not in never falling, but rising every time we fall."*
>
> CONFUCIUS

A DIFFERENT LENS

I was first alerted to the Race Across America by my friend James who was working at the BBC. I received a phone call a few weeks before the 2007 race was due to start.

He told me that he had come across this guy with six kids who was going to cycle across the States averaging 22-23 hours per day on the bike. He sounds crazy, I thought. Tell me more!

At the time I had a particular interest in producing travel and adventure documentaries and I was intrigued by the mindset of ultra-athletes. But with just a few weeks before the race was due to start, there was little chance of trying to secure a commission to produce a documentary like this, or indeed raise funds to cover the production costs. But I wanted to meet this guy.

I was living in Bristol at the time, so I travelled over to Jim's house on the other side of the country armed with a camera. The success of a film like this is dependent on two factors; the story and the character. The story sounded like it would have enough drama and intrigue, but what was this guy like?

I sat down with Jim and pointed a camera at him. He had a disarming honesty and warmth about him that immediately allayed any fears I had that the film's protagonist might lack personality.

"My mindset is extremely strong," said Jim. "I am an extremely determined individual. Whatever I've set my mind on to do, I normally achieve. I haven't had any experience in life where I've set my goal at something and not achieved it". With those words, I was convinced. I have to make this film.

For anyone undertaking the Race Across America, "the world's toughest event" there has to be an enormous amount of self-belief. Like a boxer going into battle, visualisation is hugely important and there can be no doubts about victory.

Jim had the self-belief, and his humility was exemplified in his desire to inspire others. However, I was aware that I needed to portray this sympathetically. There is a fine line between self-belief and arrogance.

The story of the documentary would hinge on Jim's personality and I was aware that the times when he was off the bike were probably the most important. This was the time where I could probe his mindset and really explore how he was feeling.

From a personal point of view, making the documentary was an honour and a thrill. Travelling across the whole of the United States at an average of 12 miles per hour was a great way to experience the varied terrain of this vast, sprawling country.

Jim's first solo Race Across America was filled with the typical moments of drama and suffering that all solo riders endure. From sickness to hallucinations, wrong turns and disagreements, my job was to capture it all. I was not a crew member, although I was closely aligned to them. But I was conscious that I wasn't helping in any way.

As the race developed and Jim's accumulated exhaustion kicked in, it was more important than ever for me to be there to capture the ensuing drama.

I vividly remember filming the crew discussion on the final night of the race. Our crew chief John had broken the news to us all that Jim was not going to complete the race within the cut-off time. The crew were despondent. I was devastated. We had come so far and Jim's story had been epic. But I was fully aware that in order for the film to be successful, we needed Jim to be an official finisher. The interest in the film is significantly diminished if it becomes about a rider who Did Not Finish (DNF).

With 13 hours left and 190 miles to go, Jim arrived at one of the final time stations with renewed vigour. We all sensed that Jim was aware of the monumental task that was in front of him. But given how he had been riding the previous night, no-one thought that he could actually achieve it.

Fifty miles down the line, things changed. As Jim's average speed increased through Pennsylvania, slowly there was a dawning realisation that this might just be possible. Everything would need to go in our favour and Jim would have to ride flawlessly, but there was an outside chance that he might achieve what none of us thought was possible.

I kept my camera rolling. It was all I could do. As Jim crossed the line with eight minutes to spare, it was a genuinely amazing thing to witness. I still don't know how he pulled it off, or where he found the reserves of energy and mental resilience on that final day to become an official finisher. But the experience taught me some valuable lessons about self-belief, mindset and the importance of completing what you set out to achieve. For that I am very grateful. Jim Rees, I salute you!

RICHARD NICHOLLS
Producer, Swift Films

*"The achievement of one goal should
be the starting point of another"*

ALEXANDER GRAHAM BELL

CHAPTER 5

Returning to Solo RAAM

Given everything that happened in 2007, most people thought that I was crazy to go back. What if I ended up with neck issues again; I wouldn't be able to improve on my previous year's finish. There were the ever-present saddle sores to look forward to, not to mention the fact that I didn't even know if I'd be able to afford to take part.

More than that was what racing again would do to my extended family. What with training and then taking part in the race itself, I just wouldn't be around that much for them.

Little did I know then the pattern I was running, what I was creating and the effect it would have on all of my important relationships. But something inside was driving me on, making me want to do it. Not only that, I decided I wanted to take three teams to America, to create interest in a not-for-profit charity I wanted to put together called Team Inspiration.

My ultimate aim was to use RAAM as a platform to inspire people to believe in their own inner greatness. This would be achieved by normal people doing something special and memorable, not just by my going quicker but by taking the biggest ever contingent to the race. I was looking to build a four-person male team and a four-person female team, along with an eight-person mixed team. It's amazing to think how quickly it all came together. Once the word got out that I was looking for riders, people appeared and the teams were formed.

The next task was to find enough people to crew for the teams. I had a large pool of friends that knew about my 2007 race and I put the feelers out. It soon became clear I wasn't going to find enough people to crew three teams, so the idea of an eight-person team was quickly dropped and we focused on putting together support crews for the two four-person teams.

I think if most of those that did sign up had known then what they found out later, they probably wouldn't have joined the crews. Even I didn't realise just how much work it was going to take in terms of planning everything. The fact that three of the female team riders and some of the crew were based in the US didn't make coordination or communication any easier. It soon dawned on me that I had perhaps bitten off more than I could chew, but the thing was in motion. I had to carry on.

Sponsorship was proving hard to come by, too. I had raised some funds from Venture Photography and a couple of other donors, but it was clear that it wasn't going to be enough to fund my solo race and cover the crew's costs. I held a crew meeting and laid out the situation. We agreed that we would all take an equal share of any shortfall so that I could race and so that they could still be part of this amazing experience. My crew consisted of Mike O'Keefe who was Co-Crew Chief, and his supporting team of Sue Yu and Catherine Rumbelow, the other team were made up of Donna von Tunk who had joint Crew Chief responsibilities with Mike, Jenn Whalley and Nicola Pendleton. We also had Mick Kelly, our dedicated RV driver.

I decided to change my approach to training. In preparation for my first solo race the year before I had ridden through the British winter. Even if it was raining, I'd still go out and ride all day. Then I'd come home, get changed and ride through the night. That approach meant that I would often be carrying a cold and would never really fully recover from it.

My 2008 preparation was all about going faster. As I built up my mileage I ended up riding with one of my best friends, Carmelo Luggeri, who is as passionate about riding his bike as he is playing his guitar with the legendary Kiki Dee. Carmelo had raced bikes for most of his life and continues to take part in time trials and races locally, and is still happy to share his wisdom with new riders young and old. Training with Carmelo meant that I was able to increase my average speed, which ultimately is what RAAM is all about. Basically, the fastest average speed wins the race. It was also obvious that I was fairly casual about my time off of the bike. I was wasting a lot of time tinkering with my equipment, a common challenge for crew members in their ongoing battle to ensure that their rider spends their time on the bike going forward rather than fiddling about with it!

At the same time as training for the 2008 RAAM, there was a global financial meltdown that had a big – and adverse – effect on my day job. Maybe I was too involved in the RAAM preparations, but I didn't see the devastating impact it would have on my industry and on my ability to provide for my family. Part of the reason for going back to go faster was to have a more compelling story to share with the corporate marketplace where I did most of my coaching and keynote speeches. Given that I was at that time a relative newcomer to the commercial coaching world, I felt that doing the world's most challenging race and going quicker would give me an opportunity to share my learning and insights, which I'd then be able to leverage to great effect with businesses.

Meanwhile, I was still attempting to find a way to keep a semblance of connection with my three kids from my first marriage. They were all growing up quickly and I was confused about how to navigate my time with them.

My eldest daughter Megan was 18 and she was in and out of contact with me at the time, as you would expect. She had her own stuff going on, with friends, boyfriends and the like. Sometimes we were close and then there would be months of no contact as she attempted to make sense of growing up with a distant father who she believed had abandoned her and her brother and younger sister. My eldest son, had chosen not to see me at all and I had to respect his wishes. I gave him what I considered to be the space he needed while leaving the door open for him to connect if he had the desire to do so. Looking back, I should have reached out to him more. He was only 16 and I shouldn't have left the onus on him to decide when and how to have a relationship with me. The same applies to my youngest daughter, she was just 11 back then, a young child on the verge of becoming a teenager. I suppose I kidded myself that she wouldn't want to spend time with her "old" dad, a man that had left her and her siblings to start a new life with a new family 150 miles away.

It is difficult for me to reflect on all of this now. I know I should have reached out more, but it was always easier then to find an excuse to be elsewhere. I'm not trying to justify my decisions. I was conflicted over the best approach to take to a very complicated situation. Of course, you beat yourself up about it, and I've cried buckets of tears over what I did and didn't do. I also realise now that, given my childhood, I was repeating a dysfunctional pattern I had learnt from my own parents. I was truly confused.

I'm sure other people who are in mixed family dynamics have had to juggle how and where to spend their time. The other complexity that crops up is whether your new partner really is committed to your other children or understands the pain you put yourself through about where your priorities are.

The choices I made all those years ago still haunt me today. A book I read some years ago called *The Only Way to Win* by Jim Loehr talks about who you become in the process of pursuing your goals. Essentially, do you become a complete arse, or do you become a better human being as you grow and learn about yourself and others? Doing what I do as a coach, I hope I've become a more rounded person over time. But that is for others to judge, not me.

Some people actually joked that I got involved in RAAM in order to get away from the family. I'm not sure I consciously did that, but I am aware that it was a way for me to escape from all of the stuff that was in my head. Being out riding meant that I didn't have to face it. I truly think I was punishing myself and that I had found a way of dampening down the noise in my head. I believe it became an addiction or a pattern for me dealing, or not dealing with, what was in front of me. Other people turn to various self-harming addictions by over-eating, doing drugs or drinking themselves into oblivion or other extremes of abuse. My vicious cycle was more subtle and less obvious to me and to others.

I also thought that at some point Tracey would be impressed with the achievement of my finishing RAAM and would be proud if I could improve on my time from the previous year. Little did I know just how far apart we were at that point from each other's core values. Even though we had discussed me taking part in RAAM again, neither of us knew the impact the financial meltdown of 2008 would have on small businesses, and what that would mean for our relationship. As I sit here now and think about what happens when two people in a relationship are not aligned in their values, while trying to manage a complex family dynamic, it seems obvious that effective communication is the key to keeping things on track. It's a little like how a small stone in your shoe can start off as a minor irritant but, if not removed, can eventually throw everything out of joint. The challenge for most of us most of the time is to take off that shoe and sort it out and not just tough it out until it's too late. This was such a big blind spot for me and it's a common issue for many of the people I've coached over the years.

When things fall apart in a relationship it is easy to side-step any responsibility and blame your partner. Of course, it is much more complicated than that. Our relationships with other people are two-way situations, but ultimately, the best you can do is to look at yourself. I knew enough about self-development at that point to realise that I could only change myself. No matter what I did, I was never going to force change on Tracey or anyone else. Change is down to the individual and their willingness to grow. But, you cannot (and you should not) force someone to change, then what you absolutely need to do is communicate with them. Back in 2008, I could not quite see this. The cracks in our relationship were starting to show, but it is only now that I recognise them and can see the patterns I was running that I did not address with Tracey.

So, that's where I was at that point in my life. From today's perspective it's easier to see now how easy it is to get stuck in a pattern that doesn't serve everyone's best interests. We are all different, with different lifestyles and upbringings. For some, especially those who have grown up with a strong family set of values, many of the decisions I was struggling to make would have been a piece of cake. Unfortunately for me, I was in a mess and couldn't see an easy way out or through this situation.

I think this is where Americans have an advantage over the British mentality. A large number of Americans have no issue with seeing a psychotherapist or psychologist to help them navigate any personal issues around relationships or just life in general. Even though I grew up in Australia, and saw the world through a very positive lens, I'm sure I could have benefitted from some guidance from a coach or mentor earlier in my adult life. I remember a GP friend of mine remarking that he couldn't believe that I was so normal, given everything that happened to me as a kid growing up. Me being me (or me being me then), I didn't give it much thought at all at the time.

The 2008 race was very different for me on a number of levels, and the same on others. For example, I was a RAAM veteran now, albeit someone who was still very new to ultra-cycling. On the other hand, I didn't have an elaborate or detailed plan when I first took part as a solo rider, and this time wasn't a lot different. Instead, I had an absolute belief that I could go quicker with no self-doubt about whether I could finish. Having said that, I still respected the event and the sheer brutal nature of the race.

People sometimes ask me: "What do you think about when you are cycling." It's a good question. The answer is: sometimes everything and sometimes nothing. On occasion, I'd be fully engaged and chatting happily with the crew; other times I'd be drifting in and out of awareness of where I was and what I was doing. There were also moments when I would become very insular and retreat into my own bubble. I'd think that the rest of the crew didn't have a clue of what I was going through mentally or physically – how could they? Every now and then I would fall into a victim mentality. I tried to snap out of that as quickly as possible as it would start to affect how I viewed the race. I would remind myself that I had chosen to compete, and needed to take full responsibility for whatever flowed from that – during and after the race.

The crew were great at keeping me interested and engaged by constantly asking questions. Mike in particular was probing why I was so keen to spread the message of Team Inspiration, and how I could gain further momentum by doing more talks to school kids across the UK. At one point, he was hanging out of the passenger window brainstorming with me, taking down my thoughts and adding his and the other crew members' ideas as I rode through Kansas.

As is normal, my energy levels ebbed and flowed throughout the race. Sometimes I felt physically strong, other times like a newborn child, powerless and with no coordination at all. A lot of this, I believe, had to do with where my mind was at the time. Your mental state can definitely affect your physical state, and negative thinking patterns will sap your energy. When I was in a good head-space I was able to cycle faster; when I wasn't as focused or in the zone my cycling speed would drop. That's not to say that the purely physical element isn't important too. It's safe to say that, no matter how mentally robust you are, the cumulative effect of sleep deprivation and cycling between 250-350 miles per day will eventually slow you down.

I was confident with my training and felt stronger as the June race date grew closer. I was consistently clocking up between 300–500 miles per week, and they were quality miles as I built towards some bigger blocks of riding in March, April and May. This year was all about riding faster and cutting out junk miles where I'd be training in all weather conditions.

Given the success of the documentary that covered my 2007 solo race, more and more people now knew about RAAM and this helped with attracting crew and gave more credibility to any potential sponsors. It also helped getting another film producer on board, with a bigger film crew, so we could document the four-person women's team and the four-person men's team as well as my solo race.

A number of meetings were held to ensure we all knew how each crew would function, and Crew Chiefs were put in place for both the four-person teams. Getting everyone on the same page regarding the logistics of travel, organisation and communication is a tricky business, even for crews that have worked together before. With so many new riders and support crew on board this time it was extremely complex, to say the least.

The women's team captain was Kerry White. Kerry had finished RAAM as a solo rider in 2007, but, unfortunately for her, outside the cut-off time. Kerry's determination to finish the race was part of her DNA. She grew up in Australia and back in 2007 she rode to raise diabetes awareness by competing as a type 1 diabetic to prove that anything is possible. I hope at some point Kerry writes about her racing experiences as I find her story inspirational and the ultra community will learn a lot from her. The other women in the team were Lauren Schrichten, a triathlete and all-round bundle of positive energy, Katie, a young Scottish rider, and Red, who was part of the mountain biking scene in Colorado. Katie was the unknown quantity. She had contacted me when she heard that I was looking for riders, and was hoping to raise the profile for people with epilepsy; in 2007 Katie won a 24-hour cycling event at Brands Hatch, which I thought gave her credibility.

The men's support crew was led by Sue, the girlfriend of one of the four-man team cyclists, Andy Irons. Riding along with Andy were: team captain Richard Newey, who had a mixed sporting background including an attempt at climbing Everest, road racer Lee Cairns from Hull, and Rick Schule from California. Apart from Rick in the US, the three other male cyclists had the chance to meet and even take a couple of short training sessions together. But nothing more than that. In truth, when it came to something like RAAM, these guys were all complete rookies, as were most of their crew. It was an interesting mix that was bound to yield some interesting stories as the race unfolded.

We had about 20 crew and riders flying over to the States from Heathrow and it was so exciting to see all of our bikes and kit being loaded as we checked in at Heathrow airport. We had a big breakfast together once all of the checks were done and we had progressed through immigration. Then, on our way to boarding the flight, I had a call from Rick Schule from California to say he had decided to pull out, leaving the four-man team short of a rider. I processed this fairly quickly and made a call straight away to Jo "Mad Dog" Maddocks. Jo had been training as part of the eight-person team we had tried to put together and had carried on riding even after we had to abandon that idea. Jo had decided to get over the disappointment of missing out on RAAM by planning to cycle from Land's End to John O'Groats.

When he took my call, Jo immediately agreed to join the four-man team instead. Crisis over, and it had taken all of ten minutes to sort it. Jo, though, was concerned that he might be the weak link in the team. But I knew that he would be a great addition to the team, even though he had never done anything like this previously. His only request to me was that I join him on his Land's End to John O'Groats ride, which he would put back until after RAAM. I happily agreed. Also, Jo's background as a psychologist would eventually play a big part in keeping the riders and the crew together and moving forward during the race. As things transpired, it was a stroke of luck that Rick had pulled out.

I had deliberately avoided coffee in the months leading up to the race, as I was hoping to use caffeine as an energy aid during the race. I'd seen some evidence to suggest that it could help. I spoke to previous RAAM winner Alan Larsen about it, but he was less sure, saying that after day two the supposed caffeine boost had little effect.

In any case, by the time we arrived in the US and were ready to race I was desperate for a coffee and decided to have one anyway with my close friend Paris Golden, who had helped me so much as part of the 2007 crew. He had planned a business trip to the States to coincide with the race start, so it was great to meet and catch up. However, as we sat there by the RAAM start line enjoying a drink, my moment of peace was quickly shattered when I received a call from Donna von Tunk. One of the crew members had seen me with the coffee and had let her know. She was furious, but I couldn't work out why.

She was just raging down the phone at me and I actually ended up in tears and had to hand the phone to Paris to see if he could calm her down. Little did I know, but Mike (co-crew chief) had keeled over at breakfast and was being treated by Donna and Catherine. This was all kept from me until a couple of days into the race, and Donna must have been under an enormous amount of stress. Mike, meanwhile, had to spend the first two days of the race hidden away while he recovered from a TIA (transient ischemic attack). It wasn't diagnosed as such at the time. Mike only found out when he returned to the UK some weeks later. He could easily have died.

My bike choice was a little different for this year's race. Following my Shermer neck issues in 2007 I had decided against a time trial bike and went instead for a climbing bike and a more relaxed set up with my main bike, which had clip-on triathlon bars and high spacers. This meant that my position from being down in the aero position to up on the hoods on my brakes were fairly similar. The wind in Kansas this year was more of a slight headwind or sidewind which made a big difference in a good way compared to a straight headwind the year before. Usually, the prevailing wind is from behind if you're lucky.

When the race started it went as planned. I had the previous year's times to measure myself against and the team was able to effectively keep a check on how I was progressing along the way. As is typical with the start of RAAM, the weather was intense. Riding into the desert was still a shock to the system, the intense heat making breathing difficult and cycling virtually impossible. Riding through the night was a little cooler, but as soon as dawn broke the searing heat started up again, so that by 8:00 am you knew you had at least another 12 hours before the temperature would begin to fall again.

I wasn't too bothered about my race position so early on in the race. You are aware of other riders around you, but fairly early on in the race you're basically on your own. You only hear about other riders' progress at the time stations, and, after a few days the pattern of the race settles down and everyone finds their level. The elite racers are off and away, while the rest of us find competitors of a similar standard to ride with. Part of the settling down process was that it gave you the opportunity to focus on the more "everyday" aspects of racing. Like saddle sores. They can play a big role in RAAM. Some riders have even had to pull out due to the pain they cause. Having ridden RAAM the year before, I knew what it felt like to try to keep sitting down on open wounds whilst cycling. It felt as though my cycling shorts had been filled with razor blades, and that with each turn of the pedals they cut deeper into my backside. Every now and then I would be able to find a blissful spot that was just off from where the saddle sores were, but, all of a sudden, the sharp pain would jolt through my whole body when the saddle found the edge of my sores again. Creams and various other treatments can help, but once you've got saddle sores it's a matter of just sucking up the pain. For 2008, I had been recommended a wound care plaster which is used for burns victims and this was one of the best bits of advice I was given. It really helped when those blisters showed up again during the race.

My 2008 race had gone pretty much to plan until I had about 400 miles to go. Then, the dreaded sleep deprivation kicked in. I began hallucinating during the night rides, and the crew had their work cut out keeping me awake and motivated. I remember one section near the end of the race when a fellow rider came up alongside me and began talking about another racer who had been killed in an accident on the stretch of road we were riding on. He suggested I stop and pay my respects, which I duly did. I climbed off my bike and just stood by the roadside in a trance-like state. I stayed that way until Donna jumped out of the follow-car and asked what I was doing. When I told her, she shook me hard and told me that I was in the Race Across America and that I was having another hallucination, the other bike rider was all in my head!

"Get back on your bike!" she ordered me. "And get back in the race!"

Later that same evening when I was climbing a set of rolling hills, I entirely forgot what I was doing and started to think that I was part of a four-person team. When the support crew in the follow-car asked me why I was not putting in as much effort as I should be, I told them they didn't know what they were talking about. This was how a four-man team operated, I said. We took it in turns to keep up the pace. At this stage I was feeling completely and utterly battered about by the night shift crew. I was getting very emotional and missed the gentle approach of the day crew of Mike, Catherine and Su.

In my hallucinatory state, I was convinced the crew in the follow-car were actually my four-man team-mates and that they were malingering while I did all the work. Once more Donna had to remind me where I was and who I was. I managed to snap out of it and I was able to carry on with a bit more focus after that.

The handover from one crew to the next took place at around 3:00 am. I had about 300 miles to go, with the Appalachian Mountains still to negotiate before I got to the finish. Within an hour of the handover I was begging Mike for a rest. For a while earlier on in the race there had been a chance I would break Mark Pattinson's British record of 9 days and 17 hours to complete the race. However, with 300 miles left I had fallen too far behind Mark's benchmark, so there was no need any more for me to drive myself too hard. I could afford to have a break after all. However, some of the crew members were upset that I wasn't putting in as much effort as I could to go faster. I reacted against this and ended up becoming childish with them in return. I was submissive and rebellious in equal measure. As I may have mentioned earlier, I sometimes had bursts of emotion that I couldn't control! I had reached a point in the race where I wasn't bothered. It's a dangerous place for anyone to be, and although I knew I would carry on and finish I had lost touch with "why" I was doing it. Mike, seeing the state I was in, emotionally and physically, agreed that I needed a long sleep and graciously let me rest up for almost three hours.

As much as I was knackered, it's fair to say that the crew were shattered as well. RAAM is one hell of a movable feast and precision is needed in terms of sleep rotations to ensure everyone is alert throughout from start to finish. I was in a dark place and had become detached from everyone. All of the things that would usually keep me engaged and focused, such as my family, vanished into the darkness of self-pity and paranoid thoughts that the crew were demons, torturing me and forcing me down deeper into hell. I was caught in a vicious cycle of thoughts that sapped my energy, rolling over as though I didn't have a choice. I knew that I did have a choice, but I just couldn't access the core positive state that I usually operated from. I was so tired that the only thing on my mind was to stop.

But I didn't stop. I did finish, and I achieved my goal of going faster than the year before. Just over 20 hours quicker, in fact. The two four-person teams did really well, too. The men's team passed me with about 200 miles to go, and the women's team finished in a time similar to mine. Following the obligatory post-race interview everybody, crew and teams, dived into a nearby bar for a well-earned beer or two.

At the top end of the race, Jure Robic had just won his fourth solo RAAM, clocking up 8 days and 23 hours. Second place went to Mark Pattinson, in 9 days and 17 hours. It was a remarkable result for his first solo race and set a new British record. Mark has since gone even faster and is one of the most second-placed riders in the history of RAAM.

Once the race was over and following a good night's sleep, I awoke to hear about some of the stories both the men's and women's teams had been through in the race. Katie had experienced a seizure fairly early on, and wasn't able to race effectively for the rest of RAAM. This had a big effect on the team's placing. After all, on paper this was a quartet that should have beaten every other women's team, but instead ended up limping to the finish line, completely exhausted. Worse still, their rookie support crew had succumbed to in-fighting and fallings out as they drove across America.

Similarly, Andy in the men's team struggled to deal with the pace and the intense weather conditions. "Mad Dog" Maddocks, who proved to be one of the stronger riders, had to step up and take on extra shifts to help the team stay competitive. There had even been a brawl within the crew, as it cracked up under the sheer pressure and intensity of the event.

Also, the RV had been involved in a collision with a tree or a telegraph pole and the follow-car was also being returned with a big dent in its side. Luckily, our insurance was fully comprehensive. We'd still be washing dishes out in America to pay off the debt otherwise.

I should have known better than to have taken such a huge cohort of riders and crew to one of the toughest races on the planet. When the dust settled, I realised that I still felt empty over what we had achieved. As soon as the race was over I felt that old urge to go back the following year and ride solo, without the distractions of organising other teams, and better my time again. All I had to do was somehow convince Tracey it was a good idea.

"The unexamined life is not worth living."

SOCRATES

CHAPTER 6

Third Time Lucky?

Arriving home after RAAM 2008, I found I had been landed with a large credit card bill, which was a combination trying to juggle the family bills and the short fall of being fully sponsored for the race. Unfortunately I had trusted a number of sponsors who had committed to supporting myself and the crew who at the last minute didn't come through.

Talk about a vicious cycle. This wasn't the first time I'd been over-trusting in a relationship. Or the second time. It was a personality trait that had been highlighted years previously when I first did a test on emotional intelligence, which I subsequently went on to become qualified in as a coach. The test showed that I had a "mistrust of others" rating of one out of ten, and that I was ten out of ten for "over-trusting". And here it was being demonstrated once again in real life, leaving me and my family under pressure to bear the financial brunt of RAAM. On the plus side, I didn't have any physical problems post-race. My neck was holding up – literally – and my hands weren't swollen. Better still: no saddle sores!

Work-wise, I had a couple of projects on the go and life seemed to be heading in the right direction after RAAM. Tracey was also looking at new business ideas to get her off the corporate treadmill, and was doing a six-month course in Gestalt psychotherapy, meaning that she spent every other weekend in London with her course group.

Relationships or marriages that survive are down to each person being supportive of one another. Those involved talk about the tough stuff and gain a deeper insight and are then better able to support each other through the dark stuff that we all have within. Tracey and I never really got to those depths as a couple. Our conversations were very superficial and we never really got to properly talk about our misaligned values. You could argue that I was in La La Land or away with the fairies, that I had a belief that everything would be OK. Until that point in my life I had been able to dodge any curveball that had been thrown at me. This is where I was stuck, I was able to support my clients and align their values but had a big blind spot around this for my own family.

I think at a subconscious level I had actually ran a pattern of fear, as a little boy growing up. I took this into adulthood, but somewhere along the way I realised that having a positive approach just made more sense. I was lucky to be surrounded by a great bunch of people in Australia who loved and supported me, friends that acted as an extended family. Although I wasn't fully aware of it at the time, these people had a big impact on me as I went from a cheeky 16-year-old kid and transitioned into a young adult.

If my goal for the 2008 RAAM had been to go faster, for 2009 it was to go faster still and also put together a crew that was perfectly aligned and excited to be taking part. The main challenge was that I had to recruit an all-rookie crew again. I simply could not expect the same people from the year before to take another three weeks out of their work and life schedules.

One of my sponsors, GL14, a local fitness chain in Letchworth, had provided me with a free membership and I ended up meeting Martyn Oakey who was the manager in charge of the gym's fitness team. We had a coffee, and before Martyn knew it he had committed to being part of the 2009 team. Within a couple of weeks, Martyn had recommended Phil Roberton, another of GL14's fitness instructors and he was keen as mustard to join.

I then met Lyndsey Springer, who worked at another one of my sponsors,

Vitabiotics, who had supported me from the first race back in 2005. Lyndsey had a nutritional background and I knew her experience would be useful, given how important nutrition is during the race. Getting that balance wrong can easily end in a DNF.

The husband and wife Quin and Sarah Speers who I knew through my connection with "Mad Dog" Jo Maddocks, and who had supported Jo and I when we rode Land's End to John O'Groats the previous year, took on RV responsibilities. This role is a key one for the smooth operation in the race. If done properly, it ensures the crews are fed and taken care of for the duration of the race. In essence, they are the team's life support system.

I had reached out to Robin who was Stateside. He had crewed for the women's team in 2008 and said he would take part as long as he could bring his girlfriend Kate into the team. I needed another team member anyway and I was happy to have her on board. The final team member was Kevin Grant, a chiropractor I had met at a conference I spoke at.

The truth is that I didn't really know why I was going back again to compete for a third time, apart from the fact that I'm extremely competitive and was in search of the perfect race where everything went smoothly.

Well, bully for me. Turns out life's not like that.

I've obviously had plenty of time to reflect, and I think that maybe I was so used to being abused as a little boy that I had grown used to being treated poorly. Now I was abusing myself by putting my body through further punishment. It sounds crazy, but I felt that I deserved to be in pain and that maybe others would have sympathy for me when they saw what I was putting myself through.

Despite the fact that I had deliberately done work on my ego over the years, maybe I had found a way or was looking for a way to get attention from those who were close to me? It's not a lot different from someone being in an abusive relationship and believing that they aren't worthy of a proper, balanced partner. It always seems to come back to having a high self-regard.

I became aware of how my low self-regard or poor self-esteem drove my ego, I would look for opportunities to chime into other people's stories about their own achievements and then hijack the conversation so I could share my own story of an even bigger achievement. A quick example of this came when I bumped into a competitor after a London triathlon (1.5 km swim, 40 km bike ride and a 10 km run). This individual was sharing how happy he was having just finished his first ever triathlon. Of course, my ego couldn't resist the opportunity of sharing just how excited I was when I had finished my first Ironman race! I didn't realise what I was doing, stealing this guy's thunder. It only hit me later, when a friend who had overheard our exchange pointed out what I'd done.

The interesting thing is that I don't believe that this person was upset or knew that I was trying to show off. It was more subtle than that but I still think about that example of how my ego took over. So many of our patterns are blind to us and we all need help seeing how these patterns can either serve us in a good way or actually be holding us back from achieving our goals.

Another aspect was that I really did feel part of the RAAM family. I was going back and re-connecting with people who knew me and people who knew what it took to finish this race. Given that I've had real issues with my identity and where I fit in, this for me was another big factor in returning time and time again. Strangely, I was leaving my family each time in search of something I couldn't see at the time that they would have been able to provide.

I was addicted to the feeling of a sense of family that RAAM seemed to give me, even though I already had two families in the UK. There's a hidden language between the solo riders, or maybe it's just a shared sense of understanding of what we go through to be at the starting line, and then what we each need to endure to get to the finish. Before the start of any race there is always a need to find some space to chill out before the mayhem starts. There's a ton of emotion flying about, and the bigger the race the more volatile the energy that builds up: excitement, nerves, anticipation, expectation, pressure, uncertainty, calm. The start line of RAAM contains all of this and more. The sense of relief when you actually begin the race is immense.

At the start of the 2009 race, Rick and Fred had invited David Goggins to introduce all of the solo racers, I remember being asked by David whether I was looking to compete for a top three place and I laughed at the thought of myself as a potential podium finisher. I did know for certain that I could go faster than previously and said as much. In 2007, I finished 18th. In 2008, I was 9th in the under-50 age category, but actually finished 13th overall. Interestingly, David mentioned that it was all about having the right mindset and I arrogantly at the time thought: what does this guy know about mindset! It was another ten years before I ended up reading his book *Can't Hurt Me,* telling the story of his childhood and his subsequent Navy SEAL career and his exploits as an ultra-runner and athlete! David's story is very powerful and shows one of the key factors that all successful people have in anything they do, whether it's school kids with great grades or sportsmen and women at the top of their game: the key determining factor is GRIT. This is also true for successful businesspeople!

Psychologist Angela Duckworth wrote a book titled *GRIT* a couple of years ago which explored what separated successful people from us mere mortals and came up with four compelling areas that were consistent:

1. To develop a fascination with what you're doing.
2. Focusing on daily improvements.
3. Ensuring you have a compelling purpose.
4. Having a growth mindset.

These successful people in all walks of life were able to create a daily routine that allowed them to stay focused and get the workout or the workload done and took control of their environment and any interference that might derail them.

Before I could get myself fully focused to start my third consecutive solo race, I made my last call home to Tracey and the kids. I tried to seem as though I was calm and relaxed but I really missed them. Some riders bring their partners, and even their kids, to the race but Tracey was very clear all along that she didn't want to see me suffer and didn't think she'd be able to handle it.

The crew had decided who was going to take the first shift, and the RV team of Quin and Sarah were with the rest of the crew to see me off at the start. It was another hot morning and Betty's Lot, which is a big parking lot in front of the beach and close to the start line, was full of follow-cars waiting their turn to fall in behind their racers.

I will always cherish the ten minutes or so I had that morning sitting with Jure, talking about his crew and life in general. As a serious competitor, he knew details of all of the racers and who his main competitors were this year. But, of course, the main person we always have to compete with is our own internal voice.

Jure didn't actually finish the race that year. For the first time in a long time he faced stiff competition from another rider, Dani Wyss from Switzerland. These two gladiators traded blows across America, swapping the lead on numerous occasions. By the time they reached the final time station, with just 51 miles to go, Dani had built up a lead over Jure that he couldn't surpass. I can't tell you why, but Jure at that point decided to pull out of RAAM. His own internal voice? Only he knows, but it just goes to show what pressure, nerves and fatigue can do to you.

As for me, I had started the race by deliberately pacing myself. It is easy to get carried away, especially at the beginning of a race when your competitive spirit is up, the adrenaline is firing and your energy tanks are full. Mix all that in with a bit of ego and the wheels can fall off very early on in RAAM. This has happened to a number of racers over the years who were expecting to compete for the win but ended up being slapped about by the weather, terrain and any physical issues that might befall a rider (saddle sores, sleep deprivation, sheer exhaustion, overuse injuries on various parts of the body, there's a huge list of things – the race takes no prisoners!).

I was riding well within myself and I wasn't bothered about my race position as I passed each time station. Once the sun set on day one I had 150 miles under my belt and knew that the crew were settling in. I had a real sense of surrendering to whatever was to come.

The temperature through that first night was still hot and it's important to keep drinking or you can become dehydrated very quickly. The other challenge riding through the night is your perceived speed. A lot of the time you think you're cycling faster than you actually are and this can have an impact on how much you push yourself.

I was already starting to recognise the route and the familiar backdrop of the Arizona desert as the sun started to rise. I was feeling strong and enjoying the view. By 8:00 am it was so hot I needed to strip off down to just my cycling shorts and short-sleeved cycling top. I took a short break to cover myself in suntan lotion and began to think about that famous RAAM paddling pool that was waiting for me and the other riders further down the road.

As the first 24 hours rounded out, I had covered 370 miles. Given the heat on day one and the amount of climbing in the first 60 miles – from sea level to 5,000 ft – that's a beast of a start. I still had another 8 hours of daytime riding on the second day and had already climbed Yarnell Grade for my third time as a solo rider. When I reached the summit I was starting to feel the lack of sleep and took my first 15-minute power nap. My plan had been to ride non-stop for the first 36 hours but the sleep demons got the better of me. My short nap did the trick and I was off again at a steady pace. My aim was to get to Flagstaff and take a longer sleep, but I first had the small matter of a nighttime climb of 6,840 ft to negotiate. I arrived safely at 2:56 am, and to trick my body clock the crew planned to wake me up again at 5:00 am as the sun was rising. This was going to be my biggest sleep of the whole race. I had decided thereafter that I would only be taking 10-30 minute power naps throughout the rest of the race.

Refreshed and energised from two hour's sleep I set out towards Tuba City with the sun keeping me warm. If you've not seen the Painted Desert, it's an amazing sight. You get your first view of the spectacular rock formations as you turn right off the main road from Flagstaff and head towards Tuba City. The Painted Desert gets its name from its multitude of colours, ranging from lavenders to shades of grey with vibrant reds, orange and pink. It is a long expanse of badland hills and buttes and, although barren and austere, it is a beautiful rainbow landscape of colours. It took millions upon millions of years for nature to create this natural canvas of unimaginable design that has been described as a multi-coloured layer cake. I hadn't really researched all the areas we would be travelling through, so when I first saw this amazing landscape it took my breath away. As I skirted along the edge of the Navajo Nation Reservation and then into their territory just before Tuba City I felt a deep spiritual connection. Maybe there was a pinch of tiredness mixed in with the elation. Nevertheless, I felt I could cry with joy and cry for all of the history I was riding through. And this was just a preamble to even more spectacular landscape coming up next: Monument Valley. The sheer majesty of its towering sandstone buttes boosts your energy – and at just the right time, too. It's the place where any rider and their crew take their most memorable race photos!

I wasn't really aware of where I was in the field at this point. Besides, it was way too early to be thinking about race standings. I was happily surprised, then, to come across fellow British rider Richard Newey, who had been part of the four-person men's team I'd put together the previous year. Richard was now racing solo, and we rode together for 15 minutes, chatting about the race and the beauty of Monument Valley. After a while,

I rode on. Not at any great pace. I just pulled away slowly, eating up the miles like Pac-Man. Knowing that the race time stations were on average 50-100 miles apart was a good target to aim for, a series of stepping stones across America. It also allowed me to check my times against last year's progress. By the time I reached time station 12 at Montezuma Creek, 719 miles into the race, I was riding in a bubble of seven other riders, all either three hours ahead of me or three hours behind.

As we checked in the crew were able to verify where everyone was. Ben Popp was three hours up the road, followed by Tony O'Keefe, Michael Cook, Franz Preihs and Claudio Clarindo – who was just seven minutes ahead of me. Richard Newey was six minutes behind me, with Jean Marc Velez and British rider Daniel Rudge further back. We continued to trade race positions as the race progressed. I was at that point 13th overall and was gutted to hear that a couple of riders had already pulled out: close friend Patrick Autissier and Scott Luikart.

As day two melted away, the next main goal was to reach the 1,000-mile point of Taos, New Mexico. To get there involved the small task of climbing through the mountains of Colorado via Cortez, Durango, Pagosa Springs and Chama. I arrived there in three days and 13 hours, soaked and cleansed from some thunderous downpours at Durango and Pagosa Springs. As I rode through Pagosa Springs I came across Franz. He was having major issues with one of his knees and had to stop every couple of hours and get his doctor to drain off excess and painful fluid build-up from his knee. The rain was a welcome relief for both of us. It was pouring so much at one point that I could hardly see five feet in front of me and had to stop for 10 minutes to let it pass. It was here in the mountains, where two ladies and a guy from one of the crews of a solo rider who had abandoned the race, greeted myself and the other solo riders with what at first I thought might have been a hallucination! The guy was on top of their van playing a blow-up guitar whilst blasting out some tunes from their van and the ladies both flashed their breasts as I rode by. It continues to make me smile to this day as I think back to that event. Luckily for me the crew in the race car behind didn't run me over as they drove by the ladies! It did brighten up my afternoon and took away any discomfort I was experiencing. I wonder whether it was after this race that RAAM changed the rules to stipulate that the support crew need to remain fully clothed!

Franz bravely carried on to Taos, where he finally had to abandon the race. This warrior told me after the race that he'd discussed with his doctor the idea of breaking some of his fingers in order to distract him from the pain in his knee. They had decided that he could probably ride with only a thumb and two fingers on each hand if it meant he would be able to carry on. This is a whole new level of pain management and I'm pleased he didn't put himself through that trauma. This is the same guy who had finished fourth the year before with a broken collarbone when he fell asleep and cycled into a road sign near Taos and decided to carry on regardless of the pain. What do these guys eat for breakfast?

Talking of food, by this stage in RAAM you are sick and tired of constantly eating gels and high-calorie snacks. Whatever happened to normal food? Then there's the creeping tiredness that overwhelms you when you least expect it. There were many moments throughout the race where I begged the crew to allow me to take a 30-minute power nap and they would negotiate me down to a 10-15 minute rest.

It's remarkable, in fact, just how refreshed you can be from a brief power nap. Then again, there are times where you've had a great nap but 30 minutes down the road you're weaving all over the place again and need to take another break.

My arrival time at Taos was 4:25 am and I was feeling the effects of the climb, as well as the beating I had taken from the storms of the previous 24 hours. The crew put me down for a long sleep of 2 hours which paid off in a big way as my speed jumped when I started riding again and I clocked up my second largest mileage of 350 miles over the next 24 hours. Even though I was able to keep up the self-motivation of riding from time station to time station, my next big goal was to reach Pratt

Kansas, 1,503 miles into the 3,000 plus miles. After that, it begins to feel like it's downhill all the way from there.

Riding through Kansas held lots of memories for me personally. It was where I developed my Shermer neck issues in 2007 and it's where you have to bring your A game to the race in terms of managing your mindset away from boredom. Kansas' long, straight roads seem to go on and on forever, with little in the way of visual stimulation to break the monotony apart from the occasional grain silo. This was also a part of the race where I struggled with nose bleeds. It was something to do with riding at altitude as you climb over the Rocky mountains and then descend from nearly 12,000 ft from the highest point of Wolf Creek Pass into Kansas, and it was uncomfortable, to say the least. It would last for hours and the only way to deal with it was to pack my nostrils with tissue paper. I looked like I'd been on a big night out and ended up in a brawl. But, if nothing else, it gave the crew something different to deal with to relieve their boredom of handing out gels and snacks whilst driving along in a follow-car at the painfully slow speed of 15 mph.

Despite my bleeding nose, I was feeling strong from my long sleep and I was able to average just under 15 mph for the next 570 miles, weaving my way through Eagles Nest, Springer, Clayton, Elkhart, Plains, Greensburg, Pratt and Maize to El Dorado, which was 1,614 miles ticked off. As a reward, I took another one-hour break off the bike to recover. Even though I had a plan of only taking power naps of 15-30 minutes after my long sleep in Flagstaff, I was now into plan D or even plan E by this stage, RAAM is all about being able to flex your plans depending on what sort of state you are in, so I was more than OK about letting the crew make those decisions based on what they were seeing. I knew I had a couple of time stations left in Kansas and the elevation was slowly descending as I headed towards Fort Scott before I crossed into Missouri, the seventh state of the race. If you're lucky you get to see the spectacular fireflies at night – along with the high humidity which is a stark contrast to the dry heat and dust of Kansas.

As I raced through the Kansas plains I started to become bloated, which is a sign of not getting enough salt. The medical term is hyponatremia, and as a result of low sodium the amount of water in your body rises and causes your cells to swell, which has an impact on your performance. I knew from experience that I needed salt to help release the fluid I had retained, but my nutritionist and I had differing views on why I was retaining water. I eventually got my way, only after a long and heated argument and many miles of riding whilst Lyndsey checked her notes.

I wasn't the only rider having problems across Kansas. I'm not sure what happened, but Christoph Strasser had pulled out of the race at Greensburg, 1,471 miles into the race, followed by Tony O'Keefe at 1,576 miles. Peter Olyer then ended his race at El Dorado, after having neck problems.

Meanwhile, I was looking forward to meeting up with Eric Johnston, who was manning the Camdenton time station. This was where the crew in 2007 made the neck brace that helped me finish the race that year. Eric was a larger-than-life fellow with a big heart. He always had a large supply of watermelons and I was really looking forward to sinking my teeth into one of them and catching up with this lovely person who I had continued to communicate with me via Facebook over the years.

It was at this same time station that a complete stranger paid for the follow-car to fill up on petrol when he found out about the race. Aren't people great?

Things got a little tense as we headed for the next time station of Jefferson City. It had been 300 miles since my last sleep, and I was really looking forward to having a break. My energy was rapidly draining away. But the crew were having their own issues that they weren't able to keep from me and this had a knock-on effect on me and my emotional state, which then impacted on my performance.

Robin and Kate, in different crews, were missing each other, and Phil and Martyn, as crew chiefs, were finding that all of their instructions were not being followed. Things were starting to implode. By the time I peeled myself off my bike at Jefferson the crews weren't in a good space at all. Before I went to sleep, I called a team meeting to attempt to resolve the tension. I was very upset that we had come 1,911 miles for things to go wrong now. It was obvious that the crews needed to change, so we reconfigured them and then I asked everyone to agree that Phil and Martyn's decisions would be followed fully from now on. There were hugs and tears all round before I went off to bed and a well-earned sleep.

When I woke, I knew I had 90 more miles to cross the Mississippi River, the 1,000 miles to go point, and into Illinois. The stretch from Jefferson City to Washington is one of the trickiest sections of the race. It has at least eight seriously steep climbs followed by steep descents, and is where I nearly crashed the previous year during the early hours of the morning when I was sleep deprived. As I followed the Missouri River to my right and the endless fields of corn, I prepared myself mentally for what was to come. I had already climbed these hills twice in my two previous solo races and this time I was feeling strong after my sleep.

Before the climbs I felt the urge to have a toilet stop, the crew pulled off the road and there was a trial and a wooded fence, so I scurried off and used the fence as a bench to sit on whilst I went about my business. I was in the middle of nowhere and there was a small dirt road near the trail and the sun was going down as a number of cars started to drive by me with my backside hanging over a fence whilst I was in the middle of my much needed number 2! What was worse was the look on one kids face! I'm pretty sure that poor kid was thinking what hell is this guy doing taking a dump out here? It looked as though I had timed my stop with some family gathering that had ended just at the point for everyone to get a view of this crazy guy in lycra crouched over a fence. I was embarrassed but more importantly I was relieved.

Maybe it was because of my mental preparation or maybe I was just feeling strong, but I found the climbs relatively easy compared to my previous memories. As day six was ending I crossed the famous Mississippi river, crossing off another big milestone on my way to the finish line. I carried on riding through the night and as I saluted another beautiful sunrise on my way from Effingham to Sullivan I began to feel tired again and needed a power nap. The crew found a shady spot on someone's driveway, but just as I closed my eyes the home owner showed up and demanded to know what the hell we were doing on his property. Phil explained that we had stopped to give me a quick sleep and was it possible for us to stay there for 30 minutes? This chap was having none of it and said he'd be back with his gun in five minutes and recommended that we needed to be gone before then. Given that I didn't fancy some buckshot in my rear end to add to my saddle sores, we packed up and I rode on to the Sullivan time station and took my nap there in the knowledge that we had dodged a bullet.

By this stage in the race, riders will have covered more miles than the Tour de France, the La Vuelta a Espana and the Giro d'Italia. I had reached these milestones within seven days of non-stop riding and with about eight hours of sleep.

I was focused and ready to put in a big shift. The weather was baking hot and dusty and the traffic was busy as I nudged further forward. I was looking forward to riding through the night and felt good as I headed towards the time station at Oxford, Ohio. There were some serious rain clouds forming above me for most of that afternoon and into the early evening, and when it came the rain was a welcome relief. As long as the crew were able to protect me from the traffic behind and light the road ahead of me, I was ready to cycle through the night.

The rain slowly got more and more ferocious, augmented by crashing thunder and furious lightning bolts. It was the most remarkable storm I have ever experienced. The crew were concerned for my safety but I was in a bubble. All I could think was, if I got hit by a lightning bolt it would be an amazing way to exit the race and a hell of a story.

As I pushed further into the night and further down the road, which was becoming more like one huge puddle, I realised I was so wet that I may as well have been sat in a slightly cold bath while I made each pedal stroke. The thunder and lightning continued to ramp up, getting worse and worse as I tried to move ahead. The crew had heard from the rest of the team who were 10 miles up the road to say that lightning had hit a power line, which had fallen and just missed their car. Phil decided that I needed to be taken off the bike to allow the storm to settle down. Usually this would be the ideal moment for a power nap, but I was wide awake, fully charged from the energy that was fuelling the storm. It was so frustrating. I was exhilarated and wanted to be out there, in raw nature, but the crew thought it was too risky. I was only off the bike for 30 minutes but it seemed like an eternity.

When I was finally allowed back into the saddle it was still raining hard but the electrical storm had calmed down. As I rode on I came to what looked like an enormous puddle covering the road. I cycled into it and it just kept getting deeper. By the time my bike was submerged up to the water bottles I realised there was no way the follow-car would be able to make it through as well. It was obvious that a river had burst its banks. The surrounding area was flooded and things were only getting worse as the rain continued to pour. The crew had phoned RAAM headquarters to let them know we were stranded and they told us we would just have to wait until it calmed down and we could carry on safely.

Once again, I couldn't take advantage of this forced stop and grab some sleep. I was just too awake and eager to press on. I wanted to get out there and ride. I also knew that the following riders would be gaining miles on me. As I sat there in the cramped follow-car, with the water level still going up, I finally accepted that I would simply have to wait things out. It was another five hours before I was able to jump back on my bike and start making progress towards the finish. Worse still, I didn't even get a time credit. Those five frustrating hours had simply been lost to the amazing storm. All of that said, and given that the layoff didn't alter my overall placing within the race, I wouldn't have missed that miracle of nature for anything. That storm will stay with me forever as one of my cherished memories of RAAM.

I still had just over 500 miles to ride and had the four steep climbs of the Appalachians and the tricky logging town of Gormania to ride through. I did a steady 250 miles before reaching the dreaded Gormania just before lunch the following day. After the previous year's fun and games dodging fully loaded 18-wheelers that seemed intent on taking me out, a different experience lay in wait for me now. My Gormania experience this time involved a couple of country bumpkins in a bright red pimped-up pick-up truck. Spotting me struggling to make my way, this pair of drooling, tobacco-chewing good ole boys, without a full working set of teeth between them, decided to have some fun at my expense.

Slowing down about 20 yards in front of me, they suddenly hit the backfire switch on their truck. I thought a bomb had gone off and I almost jumped with my bike into next week. The two rejects from the movie Deliverance thought this was the funniest thing ever – especially when they hit the backfire switch once more and got me again. Luckily for me I survived this attempt at hillbilly humour and rode on to the next time station at La Vale. This meant there were just 224 miles to go. Given my average speed to that point I knew I was going to beat my time from 2008. I also worked out that I was going to finish in sixth place overall, which I was really pleased with.

As an extra incentive, the crew motivated me further by locking me into a battle against a four-man team called Ari's Angels up and over the final climbs of the race. They kept telling me that Ari's Angels were gaining on me and that I needed to put in some extra effort to see them off. It worked. Even this late into the race my competitive nature kicked in. It completely took my mind off the difficulty of the climbs in front of me. All I wanted to do was make sure those guys coming up behind would not get past me.

Ultimately, I managed to stay ahead of them until the top of the final climb – and later got to have a beer with them at the awards banquet.

When I crossed the finish line in Annapolis I was relieved that I'd made it again, with the official time of 10 days 20 hours and 52 minutes and grateful to the team for helping me to make it across America in this remarkable race. I had slept a total of 13.5 hours for the whole race which consisted of a load of power naps of 10-30 minutes along with a couple of longer sleeps that were needed to refresh and reset my body clock. Having completed RAAM for a third time as a solo rider, going quicker on each attempt, surely, any sane person would have thought, that was that. Who would willingly submit to the physical, emotional and financial drain that RAAM puts you through? Well, I was never one to say "never". Like a lot of RAAM competitors, when someone suggests riding again you do get a certain glint in your eye.

If you've ever ran a marathon, cycled over 50 miles or done an Olympic distance triathlon, you'll know that your legs are usually sore for a few days post the event. Even going on a long trek will have a similar impact on your body.

Trying to explain what you go through physically is hard to put across to most people who haven't done sport since they left school or who have only gone to the occasional gym session.

As I mentioned previously, other RAAM solo riders fully get it and know what it takes to overcome the physical and mental exhaustion that an event that takes most competitors between 9.5 days to 13 days to finish. The average distances covered every 24 hours are between 250 - 350 miles and for the faster riders up to 400 - 450 miles, this is usually done on minimal sleep and most riders will attempt to go non-stop for the first 36 hours without a sleep!

They will then look to take between 1 and up to 3 hours maximum per 24 hours for the rest of the race, most of those sleep breaks will be divided up into power naps of 10 mins to up to a full hour, this is dependent on the state of the rider, the crew chief in conjunction with a team doctor tends to manage that aspect for the rider.

I'm sure you can remember when you've been out partying all night and gotten back in the early hours of the morning to only have a couple of hours sleep but have to get up and work that day, well I guess that feeling day in day out is how you might feel with very little sleep and with 300 miles cycling in your legs to add to the mix.

Every rider tends to lose weight over the course of the race, you're burning more calories than you can eat each day. The terrain and weather are added complications that go with cycling 3,000 miles non-stop across America, it's usually roasting hot from sunrise until late into the evening before you get any respite and some cool breeze through the night. Lots of us talk about the witching hours between 2am-6am where the temperatures can drop to below zero and it's at a time when you most want to sleep due to your body clock begging you to stop. This is a time when hallucinations usually occur but they can also get you at any point during the day as well.

I think I've briefly mentioned the saddle sores that most riders will have to deal with at some point of the race, it's one of the biggest reasons riders pull out of the race and don't finish! The pain of riding on open wounds can be unbearable at times, the only way around these is to accept that they aren't going away, you just have to manage your thoughts and dress them with numbing gels and gauzes and try to find a position on your saddle that stops the shooting pain that can rumble throughout your whole body.

This is why it's the mindset of the competitors that sets them apart from most people, they have an unshakeable emotional resilience and an ability to dig deep to complete their goal.

Will I do it again? I can't say yes and I can't say no. For me, it's a maybe.

Approaching the Mississippi bridge, 1,000 miles to go (2008)

Part way across the Mississippi (2008)

On another motorway (2008)

Andy Irons from the Team Inspiration 4 man team coming past me near Grafton (2008)

Kerry White from the Team Inspiration 4 woman team coming past me near Rouzerville (2008)

Kerry White always smiling (2008)

Getting ready for the final climbs over the Appalachian mountains (2008)

The crew couldn't stop laughing about this family of skunks, they suggested that my smell was familiar to them! (2008)

Sun burnt and tired but still smiling (2008)

Raam officials ensuring our race car is off the road (2008)

Beautiful view from the top of one of the climbs of the Appalachians (2008)

Climbing to the top of Mt Airy (2008)

Mt Airy (2008)

*Great view at the top of
Mt Airy (2008)*

*Bear hug from Mike at the
final time station (2008)*

*Team Inspiration ladies
team at the finish (2008)*

Finishers medal and a microphone in my hand (2008)

1st beer post the finish (2008)

The following morning with the crew after a good nights sleep (2008)

A tradition of ours is to take water from the sea at Oceanside and return it in Annapolis (2008)

Back to race again for the 3rd consecutive time in 2009 as a solo racer with my new crew.

Post inspection celebration, all signed off and ready to race

The mayhem of race morning in Betty's parking lot

The legend himself Jure Robic, 5 time winner of Raam solo, what a lovely human being and a truly great ultra cyclist

USA national anthem before the 2009 solo race start

The start of the first full day, just before Arizona

Arizona, those long sleeves came off just a bit further up the road, this was around 7am and it was already heating up a lot

Fellow British rider Richard Newey and I catching a 10 minute conversation as we both head towards Kayenta

Known as the 2 chimneys on the left as I cycle through the Navajo Nation

I slight uphill climb as a take a much needed sip of my energy drink

The scenery of Monument Valley is so vast and spectacular and reminds me of all of the old black and white spaghetti westerns I had seen as a kid

Yet another photo from Monument Valley

The front cover of my book and the ultimate photo of Raam apart from a good finish photo!

From right to left Lindsey, Kirsty, Phil, Me & Robin, shouldn't really stop but.......

Yes another photo of Monument Valley

Riding through a major storm in Pagosa Springs

Proof that this was not a hallucination, the race car almost ran me over!

Riding through Pagosa Springs after the storm

Focused and wide awake and taking in the stunning surroundings of the mountains

Between Jefferson City and on my way to the next time station at Washington

Riding into the light

The Mississippi bridge

Fellow Raam solo finisher and great guy Franz Preihs post 2009 finish

A family holiday in Egypt in July after finishing my 3rd Raam solo, this is Sam doing what all kids love doing

You can still see my tan lines from Raam the month before. Sam & I building mini replica's of the pyramids

My 2 sons, Elliot the eldest and his younger brother Sam

Stuart Edwards 1st Royal Marine to finish Raam in 2013, I was part of his crew.

Megan my eldest daughter & I catching up after a day working in London and enjoying a cold beer

Almost a full set of the kids together, Megan, Daisy & Sam

A very happy occasion, Megan's engagement party, Elliot, Daisy, Megan & I all dressed up

Megan & I

Daisy, Sam & Megan having fun in London

Sam & I having a great night out watching Manchester United beat Tottenham at the theatre of dreams, Old Trafford

Another fun night ice skating with Daisy & Sam in Nottingham

A very powerful reminder to live fully every day

YOUR DOG'S CALENDAR

@SEMI_RAD

					1 BEST DAY OF MY LIFE	2 BEST DAY OF MY LIFE
3 BEST DAY OF MY LIFE	4 BEST DAY OF MY LIFE	5 BEST DAY OF MY LIFE	6 BEST DAY OF MY LIFE	7 BEST DAY OF MY LIFE	8 BEST DAY OF MY LIFE	9 BEST DAY OF MY LIFE
10 BEST DAY OF MY LIFE	11 BEST DAY OF MY LIFE	12 BEST DAY OF MY LIFE	13 BEST DAY OF MY LIFE	14 BEST DAY OF MY LIFE	15 BEST DAY OF MY LIFE	16 BEST DAY OF MY LIFE
17 BEST DAY OF MY LIFE	18 BEST DAY OF MY LIFE	19 BEST DAY OF MY LIFE	20 BEST DAY OF MY LIFE	21 BEST DAY OF MY LIFE	22 BEST DAY OF MY LIFE	23 BEST DAY OF MY LIFE
24 BEST DAY OF MY LIFE	25 BEST DAY OF MY LIFE	26 BEST DAY OF MY LIFE	27 BEST DAY OF MY LIFE	28 BEST DAY OF MY LIFE	29 BEST DAY OF MY LIFE	30 BEST DAY OF MY LIFE
31 BEST DAY OF MY LIFE						

This has got to be one of my favourite pictures, the dog's calendar is a great way to live your life

December 2017 in Australia

*Craig Harper from New Zealand who I crew
chief for in 2019, he finished in 4th place overall,
an amazing athlete*

Me in my work kit

*"You cannot teach a man anything.
You can only help him discover it
within himself."*

GALILEO

SOME THOUGHTS FROM PHIL ROBERTON, CREW CHIEF FOR 2009

The Race Across America is like no other. The teams that finish the race are awesome, but the solo riders are made of something different. What they go through, both physically and mentally, is unimaginable. It's also an incredible journey for the crew.

It's not a 3,000-mile road trip, it's a deeper look at how individuals and teams react under highly stressful situations. Jim speaks a lot about his inner child. We all have them. Handling my own and being a crew chief to eight others, whose own cycles of behaviour were showing up when sleep- and nutrient-deprived, was a very profound experience for me. Even over a decade on, I'm still learning from it. So how did my RAAM story start? I was freelancing out of a gym from February 2009. I came in one morning and the gym manager at the time pointed at me and said, "You do massage don't you?". Well, Martyn was Jim's crew chief, and informed me that Jim's chiropractor had just dropped out. I confirmed my skillset, had a phone call that evening with Jim and a coffee the following week which secured my involvement in the 2009 Race Across America. Jim and I spoke a lot over the next month and he asked me to be joint crew chief.

I, of course, said yes and a few weeks later Martyn and I were in charge of a full rookie crew. We were both in our mid to late twenties and it was a baptism of fire.

After the first couple of days in the race, surviving on adrenaline, caffeine and 20 minutes' sleep, it was clear this event was something else. We'd nearly lost three members of the crew and there was certainly a divide. We kept a lot from Jim, and I spent a lot of time reassuring, managing egos, personalities and emotions. But, most importantly, keeping Jim on the road!

When you are watching your cyclist falling asleep on their bike, you are torn. This man is operating on autopilot, and he is in your care. If he's off the bike, he's not getting any closer to the finish line. This is a race. However, he also has a family back home. Being a crew chief, decisions are left to you. It does add a great level of stress.

So, after 20 minutes' sleep in the first 48 hours, I didn't sleep for more than two hours per day until we finished. I can see how sleep deprivation is used as a form of torture. Apart from obviously being tired, emotions are increased, decision making is compromised, some paranoia creeps in, and even hallucinations.

Being a crew member is tough. You don't get the limelight that a cyclist gets, but you aren't also putting your life and body on the line in the same way. It's still brutal though. A solo rider does not get across without their crew. I'd never actually been on a road bike until 2015. But it actually served me and Jim, as I had no opinions on anything cycling-related. The are no places for egos in this race, and when stress and sleep deprivation kick in, those biased opinions do come out.

Call it a "grass is greener", "victim" or "poor me" attitude, but the default when you are struggling is that you have it worse than others. There certainly is an "us vs them" mentality between crews, and for me being a performance coach, that is an itch you just can't scratch!

Unless you spend a lot of time planning and communicating from way before the race, and create systems for potential eventualities, then the phrase "flying by the seat of your pants" and having the narrative of "I wish I knew then what I know now" is very apt.

Mike Tyson famously said, "everyone has a plan until they get hit in the face." RAAM can feel like going 12 rounds with him! Ultimately it comes down to controlling your controllables. The better you manage those, and get the best understanding possible of your crew members, the better you can handle the unplanned situations that do arise.

Before the race it's like a family, and I think the riders have found such an identity. Jim feels at home with the race, and I'm confident he'll be out there again. When everyone knows who you are, and you have a "family" in charge of your life when you are at your most vulnerable, that feeling can be extremely powerful and addictive. Particularly if that unconscious mind and inner child start their noise, which will certainly be the case in an event like this.

Like everything in life, particularly in the social media highlight-reel world that we are in, people only see the tip of the iceberg. People don't see the cost and the investment. I'm not even talking about the financial cost (particularly in an event like RAAM), but the impact on other aspects of life. It impacts you physically and mentally, your work, friendships, and relationships.

There are only so many hours in the day and, whilst having goals is incredibly important, communication and awareness needs to be the priority.

Everyone sees a medal and a smile on the finish line. What they don't see is the cost! Also, the why? I'm not even sure many of these riders will be honest enough to look at 'why' they are doing this. What is really driving someone to put themselves through an event, again and again, without financial gain?

The first words I wrote were "The Race Across America is like no other". It's addictive. The solo riders have the greatest respect for each other and when they greet each other, or look each other in the eye, it's a look of knowing and understanding. I've been fortunate to crew for another successful British solo rider, so the patterns of behaviour are consistent.

I am incredibly grateful for the opportunity of RAAM, and what it has given me. Jim and I have been close friends ever since and we've both had quite the journey over this last decade. It's had a profound effect on my coaching now. If you are reading this and have a goal of getting healthy, work promotion, a new relationship, or perhaps you've just had a new addition to the family, then understand that there will be a cost to another aspect of your life. There is no problem having a goal and being selfish to reach it, but just have the awareness and honesty to own what is showing up, and know it's on you. It's on you to communicate with those close to you and regularly check in with yourself and identify the cost it's having, the why it's happening, and intervening.

Time is the most precious commodity we have, so invest wisely.

PHIL ROBERTON
Flawed Hero®

"We can complain because rose bushes have thorns, or rejoice because thorn bushes have roses."

ABRAHAM LINCOLN

Chapter 7

Reflections and Insights

In 2012, having turned my mind away for a few years from any thought of doing RAAM, I found myself agreeing to take on a co-crew chief role for Stuart Edwards, who was attempting to become the first Royal Marine to complete the race.

It was an interesting experience, getting an opportunity to take part in RAAM in a support capacity rather than as a rider – especially as we had an extremely limited budget, to say the least. It stood me in good stead for any future participation I may have in RAAM, as it means I've seen the race from both sides now and I'm better able to empathise with all people that commit to this most gruelling of sporting events. Nutty, as he's known by all of his mates, finished RAAM that year and like everyone that finishes solo RAAM, he'd give anything to go back and have another go, but as you've probably already figured, you've got to have the sponsors to be able to go back time and time again or live in America!

Having completed RAAM six times now, as a solo rider, as a team member and as part of 2 different crews, I've learned more than a little about motivation and perseverance. That, along with 20 years as an executive coach working with leaders in the fast-paced Blue Chip corporate world has given me some insights, and I believe these are well worth sharing.

Before I get into sharing some of these insights, it's worth talking about intelligence or should I say the different types of intelligence! Howard Gardner proposed back in 1983 that there were 8 and then later added a 9th.

Howard Gardner's theory of 9 types of intelligence:

1. Spatial – visualising the world in 3D;
2. Intra-personal – understanding yourself, what you feel, and what you want;
3. Linguistic – finding the right words to express what you mean ;
4. Bodily - kinesthetic, coordinating your mind with your body;
5. Interpersonal – sensing people's feelings and motives;
6. Existential, tackling the questions of why we live, and why we die;
7. Logical - mathematical, quantifying things, making hypotheses and proving them;
8. Musical – discerning sounds, their pitch, tone, rhythm, and timbre;
9. Naturalist – understanding living things and reading nature.

Most of my focus has been around the intra-personal and interpersonal aspects of being human and how that shows up in our lives, I've referred to this as Emotional Intelligence throughout my book as that has become an accepted label within the coaching world. I believe that I've covered off all of the others subtly in areas of my book apart from musical intelligence as this is not a book about signing or playing an instrument.

Although having said that, maybe I should have talked about the fact that we all need to get into a rhythm for our lives, which I believe we do – a bit like the Pied Piper we are conditioned into a rhythm of how we run our life.

Hopefully you can check in with yourself and ask whether you're using all of your potential across Gardner's 9 types of intelligence, it's worth some thought. Simply put you can chunk these into the 2 old classic ways of looking at intelligence: IQ = your Intelligence Quotient and EQ = Emotional Quotient or EI. I know from all of the research, that someone who has a high IQ and a poor EQ, will always lose against someone with a high IQ and a high EQ because they'll be smart enough to know how to use their intelligence when they interact with themselves and others. Furthermore, someone who has a high EI will be able to manage their emotions more effectively when under pressure and will be able to remain calm and access more of their potential.

A lot has been written about finding your purpose in life. We have a lot to learn from leadership gurus and spiritual teachers. It's not surprising that there are many people well into their 40s and beyond who still have not found their "thing" in life, and indeed who may have thought a great deal about what that thing is, or why they showed up on planet earth in this human form.

Personally, I drifted from school to work and from job to job without a plan as such, and I certainly didn't have a clue what I was looking to achieve. When I left school at 15, I knew that I didn't want to stay doing something that wasn't fully engaging me. But I was just marking time. I played football on the weekends and kept fit by doing 5 km and 10 km fun runs, and was happy to have what seemed like a load of money in my pocket each month so that I could go out partying with my friends when I wanted. I'd left home at 16 and was renting a room and was living very much in the moment. It's no wonder then that I didn't really stumble across my "thing" until I had turned 40 myself. I think keeping a journal helped me find my purpose. When I became a coach I started to keep a journal, among other things, noting down questions in it. In 2003, I asked myself and wrote this question in my journal: "What is my purpose?"

It took six months before an answer came into focus for me. By then I was a coach working at Speakers International. This was an organisation set up in the 1990s, originally inviting over guest speakers from America such as Tony Robbins, Brian Tracey and Stephen Covey and later branching out into setting up their own coaching events and seminars for businesses across the world. They offered a blend of mindset models that worked on mastering your motivation and challenging your beliefs about what was possible. The final part of the programme looked at taking 100% responsibility for everything that occurred in your life. It was a very powerful cocktail of mindset stuff delivered with conviction and used a clever blend of storytelling to create change with individuals, teams and organisations.

What this approach to self-knowledge teaches you is that having a purpose, or knowing what your purpose is, helps guide you in the right direction. It becomes your true north which you can steer towards. When you're on purpose, it helps you make decisions. In essence, it enables you to check whether the decisions you need to make around anything in your life are in line with your purpose or not.

I must admit, it's helped me massively on occasions when I get requests from people to get involved in various projects that aren't aligned with my purpose. I believe my own purpose is to help people with their self-confidence and self-esteem, so it's no wonder that I've ended up in a coaching role and have the ability to support charities or school children through what I do for a living. I'm passionate about what I do and really enjoy meeting new people and seeing them grow when they apply the new ways of feeling and thinking.

Once you have defined your purpose, this then shapes your identity as a person. Given my purpose of wanting to support others with their self-confidence and self-esteem, I could have become a number of things: a teacher, counsellor or therapist, but I ended up being a coach. My identity drives my values and beliefs, which in turn drives my quest to improve my capability as a coach and ensures that my behaviours are aligned while operating in the working environment.

One of the spiritual teachers I've followed for many years is Eckhart Tolle. He talks about purpose in a slightly different way, suggesting that it doesn't have to be one thing. The most important aspect to purpose is being present, so if you apply that thinking to having a purpose, it can be that you have many things that in fact become your purpose. The key to bringing your purpose to the table is being fully present in whatever you are doing in that moment. So, if you want to be a great mum or dad, be present when you're with your kids. Being present is about giving your full attention to one thing at a time, whether it's a person or a task you need to be 100% focused on or present in that moment. If you think about multi-tasking for example, you can never be 100% present to all of the things you're doing at once. Being on a call with someone whilst you are writing an email, for example, will usually result in typing errors or poorly formed paragraphs, or the person on the phone not getting all of your attention – and, let's face it, we know when someone isn't fully paying attention!

The spiritual teachers always get you to use your breath as a great way of being present. If you take a moment, stop everything you are doing and just pay attention to your breathing you become completely connected to yourself and your awareness of your breathing pattern. It's the quickest way to become present in the moment. When everything is starting to close in on you and you feel under pressure, you can become centred by just taking a moment and focussing on your breath.

Distractions or interferences take us away from being present, things like mobile phones, TV and social media. The list is long and we run patterns that take us away from being present so we don't have to face some of the things we might be struggling with, like a relationship that's stuck or a goal that's not being achieved.

At a corporate level, most organisations don't have a compelling purpose. A lot of companies have Vision and Mission statements that fall a long way short of defining a purpose or having a big why they do what they do as a business. Over the years I have facilitated a number of three-day workshops to help leaders craft and wordsmith their purpose statement. It has a massive impact when it's done properly and shared with the rest of the organisation. It helps by thinking about purpose as, "What is the organisational legacy going to be long term?" and it is more profound if it impacts more than just the employees and business performance but actually goes out into a bigger context and makes a difference in the local, regional, national and global community.

Usually, companies have a vision of becoming number one in their industry, or having a certain turnover by a certain date, and that's all well and good. But it doesn't really motivate or connect the individuals that are out there selling the products and the services of their company.

Being connected to a purpose adds meaning to why you do what you do and will give you extra motivation when you're having a tough day.

Whenever I've competed in Ironman triathlons or the Race Across America, I've been able to tap into my deep sense of inspiring others to believe in their own inner greatness by attempting to show them what is possible with the right mindset.

Your purpose drives who you become (your identity) which then drives the values that in turn have an impact on how you behave with yourself and others.

In Eckhart Tolle's book, *A New Earth*, he talks about the three things we need to focus on as human beings: Acceptance, Enjoyment and Enthusiasm. Of the three things, I have found Acceptance to be one of the tougher ones to master, being able to accept what is happening in your life, especially when you feel you have little choice or control over what is in front of you. It took me a good couple of years to start accepting the breakdown of my marriage with Tracey. When I look around, it appears that a lot of us struggle with this concept of acceptance, we tend to get stuck in thinking that whatever we're experiencing shouldn't be happening! We stay arguing with reality and that ends up with us becoming stuck in a vicious cycle. Was there a way out of me being stuck? Yes there was but it was a blind spot for me that kept me stuck for longer than I needed to be. I thought I could find the answers through reading various books and looking at myself in a reflective manner! It took a friend to tell me that I couldn't sort through some of the big bits of emotion that I was trying to navigate myself through, I needed help and I had to go in search of someone I could trust to help me understand and eventually accept what I had been struggling with for a number of years!

Patterns of Behaviour

In coaching or therapy, what the person is looking for are patterns of behaviour that you run in your life. We all run patterns that either help or hinder us!

The first step is to become aware of what those patterns are and how they are showing up. In my coaching practice I use an Emotional Intelligence questionnaire which explores 16 different scales and looks at how you self-manage yourself and how you manage yourself with others. It also helps you see any potential blind spots. I find it funny when I ask people what their blind spots are and they attempt to answer the question! Blind spots are blind to us and we operate out of awareness. My big blind spot was around the misaligned values between myself and Tracey, which ultimately caused the wheels to fall off of a 17-year relationship.

You can quickly find out your behaviours by doing the values exercise at the end of this book. I'd recommend that if you're in a relationship, you both complete it separately and then compare your results. Most relationships that end up breaking down do so because of a lack of alignment in values. By completing the exercise you'll be able to explore how you can both navigate towards each other, or at least fully understand why you act and behave in the ways you do.

Feeling/Thinking

What we're thinking drives how we feel about every event or interaction we have with ourselves and others. This can be simply put by thinking about the lens we see the world through, whether we're optimistic or pessimistic. Put another way, it's about whether you are typically positive or negative in how you see things. How you view the world has an impact on the results that show up in your life.

Neuroscience has shown us how powerful this is in terms of our health and wellbeing. Bruce Lipton has researched this area extensively and has written about it in his book, *The Biology of Belief*. Every word we use in our internal dialogue with ourselves has an energy that goes with it, which causes emotion or how we feel; the same is true when we communicate with others, depending on our emotional state. Those words whether they're positive or negative will cause a chemical cascade that will have an impact on our body. Someone that is negatively charged for most of their lives can end up being at dis-ease with themselves and others and it's no wonder that they end up stressed and manifesting a disease of some kind! Read Bruce's book if you want the data but this is how most disease is caused by us!

Another way of thinking about the lens we see things through is a story of a farmer and his horse. Its origin is unknown but it comes from the Taoist tradition, so it could easily be more than 2,000 years old. And even though that's about as old as stories get, this one is completely relevant to your life and how you can live in the future.

One day the farmer's horse runs away. When his neighbour comes over to commiserate the farmer says: "Who knows what's good or bad?"

The neighbour is confused because this is clearly terrible. The horse is the most valuable thing the farmer owns.

But the horse comes back the next day and he brings with him 12 feral horses.

The neighbour comes back over to celebrate: "Congratulations on your great fortune!" And the farmer replies again: "Who knows what's good or bad?"

And the next day the farmer's son is taming one of the wild horses and when he's thrown from it, he breaks his leg. The neighbour comes back over. "I'm so sorry about your son," he says. The farmer repeats: "Who knows what's good or bad?"

Sure enough, the next day the army comes through the village, conscripting able-bodied young men to go and fight in a war – and the son is spared because of his broken leg.

And so this story can continue indefinitely. Good. Bad. Who knows?

But what's the point?

We tend to label things that happen in our lives as good or bad. I've certainly been caught in that thinking a number of times when things haven't gone the way I planned them. It's usually only with reflection that you can see the opportunity for growth within the experience, and it's certainly a healthier way of seeing the things that show up throughout our day. From birth to death, life is all about learning. If something happens, good or bad, you should look to learn from it and grow.

So, if we can free ourselves of judging everything and everyone, including ourselves, we can free ourselves from a load of stress and unhappiness.

A great question to ask yourself, is when are you going to be happy? I've asked this question to thousands of people over the years and the answers tend to be fairly similar. People often say that they'll be happy when the mortgage is paid off or when they're debt free or when they retire or when the kids leave home! Lots of interesting responses and most of them are years in advance of the day the question is being asked!

Most people are putting off their happiness for a future time when things have been achieved, that's chasing happiness instead of being happy now!

That approach is like trying to pick up a bar of wet soap in the shower, every time you go to grab it, it slips out of your hand!

Byron Katie's book *Loving What Is* talks about how when you argue with reality you only ever lose 100% of the time! So many of the spiritual teachers talk about just sitting with whatever is in front of you and being present to the opportunity of learning and growing. Sometimes, especially when something terrible happens (which is a judgement), we get upset and spiral out of control. We end up leaking energy on things over which we have no control.

We all have a certain amount of life-force or energy available and we need to ask ourselves whether it's worth spending energy on some of the things that we get caught up in throughout our day. A lot of the time we end up getting really stressed or anxious about tiny little things that really aren't worth our attention.

The old classic mantra of "This too shall pass" is so true when we look at these events. Nothing lasts forever: even if it seems like you're going through hell it doesn't ever keep on with the same intensity. Staying focused on what you want as your desired outcome is important and will help ensure you don't get caught up in a negative pattern.

When I speak to my kids and ask them how their day has been, every now and then one of them will tell me they've had a bad day! When I ask what has happened, they usually tell me about an incident that occurred in the morning which then overshadowed the rest of the day. One event in our day doesn't mean we've had a full day of bad things happening. What tends to happen is that we take that bad moment and continue to chew it over and over again, which then in turn keeps us stuck in a negative pattern.

I've already touched on how we end up forming an attachment to our identity or to the various identities we give ourselves, sometimes it's about the journey we've been on and sometimes it's about the result that you've been pursuing and sometimes it's none of the above and it never ends, until you're dead!

Identity is a funny thing. Just when you think you've defined yourself through something you've done or through a role you've played as a husband or wife or as a professional athlete or business person, life will throw something at you that will create another chapter to challenge you. It's all about getting outside of your comfort zone. Until you do, you'll never know what you are truly capable of.

I've met a lot of people who have struggled with who they are when the children have grown up and left the family home and stepped out into the world on their own. All of a sudden their identity of being Mum or Dad has been diminished and they fall into a great void of not knowing who they are now. The same is true with a leader who either retires or is made redundant. They will have spent so many years playing their role that, when they no longer have their title, they start to question who they are now.

Our identity or self-concept is shaped from childhood and continues to evolve throughout our lives. Maybe a better goal for ourselves is to shape our identity around being a gentle, loving, caring human being. Knowing who you are and what you stand for will help you stay centred and have clarity in everything you do.

"Each player must accept the cards life deals him or her: but once they are in hand, he or she alone must decide how to play the cards in order to win the game."

VOLTAIRE

CHAPTER 8

Validation

I realise now that a lot of what drove me to push myself to such extremes by firstly competing in Ironman events and then going longer by competing in RAAM, was that I was hoping for validation from others. To show that I was worthy, that I had accomplished something that merited praise or recognition.

There was something deep within that drove me to look for this. I felt that I wasn't getting this in the intimate relationships I had with my family, so I looked for it elsewhere. My inner child was driving a pattern of behaviour that was like a wrecking ball with the important relationships in my life. The little boy that had never really felt safe and loved was, unbeknownst to me, causing chaos. At this point in my life, I was creating from fear.

This vicious cycle was a deep pattern that I was running and it was a massive blind spot. We all have blind spots and this one had been driving a bulldozer through my life since my early childhood. I was operating without awareness of the impact I was having on those closest to me.

Creating from fear is a very unstable base. You're on very thin ice and you cannot achieve or tap into your fullest potential when operating out of fear. When you're in fear, you end up attracting more fear into your world and that turns into a vicious cycle that drives more of what you don't want into your life.

Here's a quick example of how fear can attract the very thing you are in fear of; if you're in a major city for the first time late at night and you're worried about being mugged, you will walk down that street nervous and worried that someone might mug you! A robber looking to mug someone is looking for exactly the sort of person you become by being nervous and worried; your fear drives the very behaviour that the robber is looking for! This same pattern is playing out in other scenarios in our lives, so we need to be constantly aware of how we are showing up in every situation.

It's crazy for me to think that most people who grow up with a strong set of values from their parents never need to go out of their way to seek further validation beyond their family unit. Most people would be happy and fulfilled knowing that they were a great parent who supported their children. For me, it was very different. I didn't have those deep-seated values to help me understand what "good" looked like around a family dynamic. As much as I wanted to be part of my own family, I hadn't been shown what a healthy family set-up looked like by my parents.

Another perspective that I learnt through therapy is that chaos was my "normal" growing up. It's what I became familiar with and felt that I deserved. So even though I was desperate to be part of a normal family environment, I was unconsciously creating a chaotic life because that's what I was used to. My pursuit of doing extreme events was my way of proving I was tough enough to handle anything that was thrown at me, that I was unbreakable. This drove an unquenchable thirst to put myself in dark places physically and emotionally.

As a little boy, I grew up in fear and was worried about being abandoned and it skewed my family values. I'm not looking to blame my parents, I'm just attempting to help you see that these things matter when you're building your own family values for your own children to grow up with. There's a great chapter in Angela Duckworth's book *Grit*, called Parenting for Grit and it shows some of the research around how to best support your children. In the fast-paced world we live in now, where we are constantly connected digitally through email, Twitter, Instagram and every other form of social media, we've actually become less connected personally and even more distant from the very people we should be close to! I think we've sleepwalked into this new way of what we believe is connecting, but it avoids the very thing we all need which is physical connection and a hug. I've seen whole families at a restaurant with the parents on their phones and the kids on tablets playing games as they wait for their meals to be served. No one is talking to each other!

On reflection, I know for sure that I was looking for attention but it was my inner child driving my subconscious mind to seek what I didn't feel I was getting from my family. Even if I was getting their love, it wasn't showing up in a form that I could see.

This is common in relationship issues. One partner may want to be cuddled and close to their other half to feel loved and safe, while the other partner may want just to be settled in their house together, to feel safe and loved. This pattern, along with many others where values are misaligned, can have a dreadful effect on a relationship. For me, I know my wife and I were misaligned around finance. Money was never a big deal for me as a young boy, maybe because we were never really rolling in it when I grew up. My family lived from one month to the next, like most families still do today.

So, here we were, Tracey and I, in a relationship for 17 years and bumbling along and unaware of each other's values and how that was impacting the both of us in very different ways.

Our values weren't aligned and we never explored or addressed this. I want to make it clear that I'm not judging my values as the right set of values versus Tracey's values, they were just different and we drifted. I was stunned when we split up and couldn't believe what was happening or why it had come to an end. The first six months were brutal as I started to realise the full extent of what this all meant. The family that I had been focusing on for the past 17 years had just evaporated in front of me. Apart from our son Sam, the rest of the family was simply deleted.

I know this is not unusual in lots of separations and can vary from being very amicable to the other end of the spectrum where it's hostile and vile. I only hope that if you are going through a separation that you do everything you can in your power to ensure that you both have open communication and seek mediation so that you can remain civil through what is a tough situation for all concerned, especially the kids and extended family.

I remember having a couples' therapy session in the first year of our separation, I was concerned about the impact this would have on Sam.

The therapist very quickly got into the fact that this wasn't about Sam, it was about the two of us and our inner fears from our childhoods! For the first time we both sat there with tears streaming down our faces, listening to each other explaining how our inner child was terrified.

The therapist asked me to recount my childhood memories. I was still reeling from having just heard Tracey speak for the first time about what she most feared and I was almost speechless as it started to all make sense. I had done a good job of burying a lot of my early childhood memories and most of the time I would suggest that I had an amazing childhood, but that's not the truth. As a little boy growing up I remember my Dad working at one of the local factories and my Mum would typically have a local cleaning job at a school or office. I'd be cared for with meals on the table but my parents' relationship was old school and very much along the lines of the dominant male figure and submissive mother. I felt loved by my mum, but it was their relationship that shaped me as a little boy growing up. They often argued, usually fuelled by drinking and this ended up leading to Mum on several occasions attempting to escape by just leaving and running away, sometimes for weeks before Dad eventually tracked her down and talked her into coming back. I didn't know it at the time but this fuelled my fear of being abandoned and it created a pattern for me as a little boy and into my adult life which I took into my relationships and it is sprinkled throughout my life.

So as we sat there with the therapist I started to realise that we had over time fed each other's fears. Tracey was worried about our finances and to her own detriment was trying to support me and our family and her parents, because that's all she knew. Not that I wanted to, but I ended up playing the perfect role of feeding her fear of having no money due to the nature of running my own business which was feast and famine in its nature. On top of that, I was blindly addicted to competing in ultra-events like RAAM, and at the time, I didn't realise that my inner child was running the show. The sense of who I was at that point was wrapped up in my identity of being an ultra-athlete instead of being a breadwinner. This in turn eroded Tracey's trust in my ability to support and provide for the family.

Another layer to this pattern was that I desperately wanted Tracey to believe in my ability to grow a successful coaching business and when this never came from her, it was like Kryptonite to me. I wanted the woman I loved and adored to believe I could do it and this had a paralysing effect on me.

But the mirror that Tracey was reflecting back at me was all about me needing to believe in myself and my ability to have a successful business. Weirdly, it was never about whether Tracey believed in me. The business started taking off when I was on my own and I realised that it was now or never. Leaving the 5-bedroom family home and then living in a converted garage can be a real leveller! I had to start believing in my own inner greatness which had been dampened down for years from having a low self-regard and self-confidence. I got caught up in thinking that I wasn't worthy and that I wasn't good enough to be successful as a coach and got stuck for a while believing I was an imposter. The very thing that was my big message to others about believing in their inner greatness was something I too needed to deal with. This is a deep-seated belief of mine that everyone has greatness inside them and was what I was all about and I was passionately doing everything I could to prove it to others.

In Gregg Braden's book *The Divine Matrix* he talks about the three main fears we all face and they all seem to play out for all of us throughout our lives in varying degrees.

The three fears are: Fear of Separation-Abandonment; Fear of Low Self-Worth; and Fear of Surrender and Trust.

For me they are all woven into every relationship I can remember. The biggest challenge I've had is obvious now I can see it, but being abandoned as a little boy did have a big impact. We all struggle with separation and abandonment at a spiritual level. If you buy into the thought of oneness, we all come from the source and return to it after our time on earth, so that sense of longing and separation is in all of us.

The neuroscience world has continued to show us that the world is a mirror and it reflects back to us what we think and feel. This is where big gains can be made if we work on ourselves and our beliefs of what is possible and whether we deserve to be happy.

The second fear is something I see a lot in people I have coached over the years and it's the main reason I do what I do. I've already shared that I have a passionate belief that we are all built for greatness. Low self-worth has played a role with me and it's no surprise that here I am attempting to help others to see their inner greatness, and yet I have continued to struggle with my own! The slightest chinks you have in your ability to have what you want in your life will be traced back to your own lack of self-worth. The mirror is at work on your behalf.

The final main fear of surrender and trust has an impact on how safe we feel in our intimate relationships and the world we live in. Again, if you get caught up in the fear that is driven by media which churns out murder, rape, abuse, weather disasters, broken marriages, suicides, predictions of the next financial crash and so on, then it's no wonder that we end up feeling nervous and have a lack of trust that things will work out and it will all be OK.

> *"Life is a mirror and will reflect back to the thinker what he thinks into it."*

> ERNEST HOLMES

Our true beliefs show up in our most intimate relationships. These are mirrored back to us, giving us the opportunity to grow and heal the painful feelings of the past. We need to explore the patterns that allow hurt to exist in our lives so that we can be happy in the now.

Again, all of this is easy to see with hindsight. It's not obvious when you're in the middle of it all, everything becomes a fog when you're juggling a full-time job and supporting a young family. I emphasise that a lot of this happened because I had blind spots. I was running patterns of behaviour that weren't rooted in solid family values and I do recognise that there were periods where I was self-obsessed and yet I was completely out of awareness. The crazy thing is, that I thought that I should have these things nailed down and completely sorted and yet even though I've read extensively and been on loads of courses and coached others around their values and patterns of behaviour, I was blind to some of my own stuff that needed attention.

I wasn't seeing the cause and effect, because Tracey was supporting me staying stuck in the pattern that I and we were stuck in. Neither of us could communicate our deeper fears, which allowed the pattern to play out and our deepest fears were eventually revealed.

I've shared all of this personal stuff to shine a light on what happens when as a couple your values aren't aligned. It's an extreme example, but what happened between us, shows that, whatever life throws at you, it's important to talk, to communicate and respect each other's feelings. The only people who know the truth are the two people within the relationship. And even then there are always two versions of the story, and somewhere within those two stories lies the real truth.

I look back with a fragile heart and it's only now that I can truly see the struggle we both went through, doing our best with what we knew at the time. What I do know is that we bleed our worries and fears onto the person closest to us. I wasn't strong enough to show my own vulnerability and that I too was struggling to process what was going on within our relationship, which in turn meant that I didn't handle my own emotions very well, as I was scared of losing Tracey for good.

When you bury that stuff, I believe it weighs you down further by adding to other aspects of your inner darkness and it becomes another thing that you can beat yourself up with in the future.

It's been four years since Tracey asked me to leave and I'm still not fully over it. I've come to realise that I don't want to get over it and leave it in a box, all of those beautiful memories we shared together as a family as the children grew. Maybe I'm fooling myself with my positive mindset and the way I look at life, but I'm always going to look at that time as a couple juggling life together as a gift.

My extreme positive mindset still believed that somehow she would turn around and ask me to come back but the truth is we were on a path that has destroyed any chance of that happening. We locked horns and ended up in court in an attempt to sort out what we each thought was a fair settlement of our assets.

I can now see and own the decisions I took throughout my adult life and only with deep reflection and insight, which includes help from close friends, family and therapy, I can now see what I was never going to see whilst I was in the thick of it all. As I was running towards trying to wake other people up to believe in their inner greatness by competing in extreme events, I was also running away from the emotional turmoil of my dark passenger, that little boy who didn't know any different!

You've probably read somewhere that people come into your life for one of three things:

A Reason, perhaps to help you grow and learn something; A Season, for a period of time in your life that you both needed to be together; or A Lifetime, which is fairly obvious what that means. We only get disappointed and upset if we try and force them beyond their purpose.

Like most human beings, I have struggled with accepting the change. This ending has beaten me down to some of the lowest places I've been in during my adult years and yet I can see myself emerging out of that darkness. I've found strength in knowing that I'm a caring and loving person that made some mistakes and got it wrong some of the time around some of the important stuff. I doubt there are many people on the planet, who with deep hindsight could say they got it all right all of the time. We all do our best with what we know at that point in time.

I still admire Tracey and I will always hold a place in my heart for her.

Millions of marriages break down every year and it can get very messy when you have a blended family dynamic, where kids end up choosing sides. It can be brutal.

I think I'm a better human being as a result of those struggles and scars and I'm certainly a better Dad for my kids who are all adults now. It has certainly given me a very different perspective on the struggles others go through when a relationship breaks down which has helped in my coaching practice.

Having said that, I wish I had watched the American TV drama called *This Is Us 30 Years Ago* before I had become a parent. The drama series covers every aspect of the complex family dynamics that unfold in most people's lives. Without giving away too much, the story revolves around a young couple who fall in love, get married, settle down and eventually have a family. Jack is the father in the story and he is an amazing example of a committed parent and husband and would have been a great role model for me as a young father. Watching the programme I found myself giving myself a hard time for not being more like Jack and yet, here's the thing: Jack also had his own demons and darkness that he struggled with from his own childhood which was a blind spot for him. As much as Jack didn't want to repeat his own father's patterns of behaviour and did everything he could to avoid history repeating itself, he ended up through a series of struggles succumbing to the same darkness his father struggled with.

I'm not suggesting we live our lives through TV dramas, but some of us really do need help to see what the important family values are so we can be more aware to pass those on to our children.

I really need to over-emphasise that even though this is so obvious for so many people reading this book, if these family values are not in place it's very easy to see how much chaos can be created in every aspect of your life.

For me, I never really had a normal upbringing and this ended up having a massive impact on my own family dynamics in both marriages. It's so important to know what "good" looks like, even more so in the diverse way in which modern society has evolved.

I thought that I could work through all of this by myself until a close friend challenged me. In a good way, he just straight out asked if I was getting any help. He knew that there was no way I could sift through this and work on myself. I had a pattern of constantly searching for answers and insights in books or some of the courses I would put myself on to learn and grow. But that wasn't working and I had stayed stuck for a long period of time. That nudge was what I needed.

I remember watching the TV hit Billions where Wendy the coach/therapist said this: "The thought that someone might know that you need help, is worse than not getting the help you need."

I had sat with this stuff, trying to tough it out, and was really bad at asking for help until my friend pushed me. Some years ago I got heavily involved in a charity called Cycle Against Suicide over in Ireland, founded by Jim Breen. The charity's slogan was "It's OK not to be OK, and it's absolutely OK to ask for help."

Here in the UK, we are really poor at looking for support, whether it's getting a coach to help you tap into your full potential or a therapist to support you with some of the tougher stuff. I hope you can learn from my insights even though my ego would suggest I thought I had it sorted! It's obvious I didn't and I hope you have the courage to take that step to seek help if you're struggling.

All of this stuff around change and in particular changing yourself and allowing the better version of yourself to show up can be tricky. I have a saying that I share a lot with those that need to hear it: "It's easy to do, it's just easier not to!"

It's easy to drop a few pounds if you're looking to lose weight, the challenge for most people, is that it's easier not to have to change your eating and exercise habits.

There are so many things that can get in the way and stop us from taking the action we need to take, it's so easy to fall into the thinking that it can wait until tomorrow. Whatever your goal, just take the first step towards it and then create healthy habits to ensure you are consistent so you can stay on track.

"What lies between us and what lies ahead of us are tiny matters compared to what lies within us."

RALPH WALDO EMERSON

CHAPTER 9

What Fingerprint will you leave?

There are various coaching models that I use when working with leaders and their teams that I have learnt over the years. I believe my fingerprint metaphor that I use to create awareness with individuals and teams is one of the most powerful. I usually use a glass of water to explain this, so if you imagine picking up a glass, each time you touch it you leave behind your personal fingerprint.

Now, depending on how emotionally intelligent you are you will leave a different fingerprint on the glass each time. For example, if you have really high emotional intelligence where you are very self-aware and aware of others, and your interactions with others are really mindful, you'll pick the glass up and leave a positive fingerprint on it. If you have mediocre emotional intelligence, some days you'll be good and some days you'll be operating completely out of awareness, unaware you'll pick the glass up and sometimes leave a positive fingerprint on it and sometimes your touch will crack the glass. Finally, if you have really poor emotional intelligence, you'll be completely out of awareness of the impact you're having on others and it's highly likely you will pick the glass up and potentially shatter it.

When I share this metaphor with a team and ask them if they've got examples in their careers where they've had a boss who has been poor at giving feedback or interacting at a personal level, I always get lots of people saying yes. Exceptional leaders score high in emotional intelligence.

The data is overwhelming. Their ability to interact and engage at a human level is extremely powerful. They can hold a room full of people. There's an energy and self-confidence that is obvious. These individuals typically have a high self-regard and a high regard for other people. These are the two aspects which are fundamental to being a balanced human being and they have a big impact on the rest of what makes a high performer in any industry or profession.

In every interaction we have with another person, we leave our unique imprint on that person. Every conversation, every look no matter how subtle, we leave our fingerprint. It could be a tut or a sigh. It doesn't matter: we have just left a fingerprint with that person. We've all had situations in our lives where we have spent time with a friend or a colleague and been really present, giving our full attention. As a result, that person will receive a huge boost from the interaction because of the positive fingerprint you left with them. Similarly, there will be situations where we weren't present at all and have left some people in a worse state.

The whole point with the fingerprint metaphor is that it's about having a heightened awareness and deliberately leaving a more positive impression because you can.

Even though this is something I share with leaders and everyone I come into contact with, I definitely don't get it right all of the time! Some time ago I was working with a leader and their team doing some team development and that morning I had been sharing with them the fingerprint metaphor and I asked them to start paying attention to all of their interactions with others.

We went for a lunch break and on this occasion, lunch wasn't provided, so I went to a local store and got a sandwich and some fruit and some snacks for the group for the afternoon. As the young lady was scanning my stuff through, she was asking me various questions about whether I wanted to take advantage of the offers they had on some of the items I was buying, as she was asking the questions I was waiting to be checked out and was busy checking my emails that I hadn't seen since the morning! As I was looking down at my phone and without looking up, I answered a series of nos to the young lady, I was completely out of awareness, until she asked if I wanted to marry her!

It caused me to stop immediately and snap back into being present with her, she obviously was only joking but it was a beautiful gift of awareness from her. I blushed and laughed at the same time and then thanked her for bringing me back to being present with her. I told her what I did for a living and that I had higher standards for myself but I was grateful for her reflecting the mirror back at me. We laughed together and I parted from the shop having just learnt a beautiful lesson from a complete stranger, of course it was a great story to share with the team I was working with when we got back together post our lunch break.

There are three areas in our lives we need to pay attention to regarding the fingerprints we leave in all of our interactions with others. The first of these is the one I believe to be the most important.

Intimate relationships

I think we can fall into a trap with the people who are closest to us, who know us better than anyone else. We tend to take our wife or husband, kids, siblings, parents and really close friends for granted. It's not on purpose that we do this; it's out of an awareness of just how important they are in our lives. They are like our life support system and we need to raise our game when we're with them.

It's so easy to get caught up in the grind of everyday life and lose track of how we are showing up with the people who mean the most to us. Simple things like taking your kids to school or dropping them off for a night out with their friends mean a lot. And we need to be present and aware enough to let those people know that when we drop them off or take them to school it's not an inconvenience or that we expect anything in return. We are doing it just to spend time with the people that are important to us.

I remember times when I'd get back home from work and still have urgent emails to send. As I walked through the door I'd be distracted, ignoring my kids who'd been waiting all day for me to come home so that they can share some exciting news about their day at school, or just have a cuddle. Then, when I've sent my emails I go back to my kids and ask them to tell me about their day, only to find that the moment has gone. It's lost. You are lost in a pattern that hasn't served you well.

Work colleagues

A big chunk of our lives will be spent with work colleagues and other professionals, so we need to raise our game with them too. Being aware of how you're showing up is so critical. We only have one opportunity to make a good first impression and leave a positive fingerprint. There are some occasions where you might be coming from a meeting where you haven't had the result you were hoping for, or perhaps you might have been hauled over the coals for something and you show up at the next meeting with some of that negative energy.

This is a big area for leaders to be mindful around. The fingerprint you leave in all of these interactions is important and will ripple through your team or leave an imprint on an individual. Your team will constantly be looking for cues, looking for chinks, hanging off every word you say and how you say it. In essence, they are looking to see if what you are saying matches up with how you're showing up. Are you being authentic?

Leaders who do this really well have a high self-awareness coupled with a high awareness of how others are responding and can calibrate how they engage with each of their team members and other work colleagues. When a leader has low emotional intelligence, their transactions have poor outcomes: team members don't share because they don't trust their boss and then the leader can easily misinterpret the signals they are receiving from their team members. They end up blaming their team for the lack of engagement or performance and are operating completely out of awareness of the fingerprint they are leaving.

It's a common scenario where I'm coaching a leader and they end up realising that it's the way they have been communicating with an individual in their team that is causing the issue.

When we judge others, there's an energy that goes with that judgement. We end up closing down how we expect that person to behave, and only see what we expect to see and hear from them. Given that language is all we have, there will be certain words we use in these interactions that will keep us stuck in disagreement.

So, once again, we need to slow down and raise our awareness in these situations to ensure we have better quality working relationships.

The impact of low engagement is fairly obvious with poor performance, staff turnover, stress and potential long-term sickness – all linking back to a leader with low emotional intelligence!

The rest of the world

So, I've covered off our intimate relationships and our work colleagues. Now for the final group of people we bump up against: the rest of the world! This is where we could have a massive positive impact if we all leave a positive fingerprint in all of our interactions, big and small.

This is an area I'm passionate about. These interactions are important. We don't really give them much thought but they really do matter. I'm talking about the person on the checkout at your local store who you could easily dismiss as not worthy of your attention, like the example I gave earlier, or the person serving your meal at a restaurant, or even the person you are squashed against on a busy commute. These are all opportunities to leave a positive fingerprint. Just a simple smile is better than no connection at all. That small smile might just lift that person enough for them to feel better about themselves which then has a positive impact on the rest of their day and the people they interact with. And it all began with the small positive fingerprint/smile you shared with a complete stranger.

Finally, here's the thing with leaving a positive fingerprint, all of us will have inspired loads of people in our lifetime, most of those people will never have given you feedback on the impact you've had on them! We will also have some people who would prefer not to bump into us ever again. Every now and then I've had people I've coached give me credit for transforming their life and it does make you feel great when someone takes the time to share their thoughts.

Here's a short note sent via email from Jon Shubert who has cycled around the world and then won the UK national 24-hour time trial just 6 weeks after returning home and then more recently, has set a new world record for cycling 100 miles in under 3 hours!

Since the wheel was invented, no one in all of recorded time has ever been able to go that fast on a bike, it's a similar achievement to the British runner Roger Bannister, becoming the first person who broke the 4-minute mile and more recently the Kenyan runner Eliud Kipchoge who broke the 2-hour barrier for running the distance of a marathon.

> *Hey Jim*
>
> *I'm so grateful that we have connected recently. I was in awe of you (I still am) when I was a teenager, and it was a bit like meeting cycling's David Beckham when I ran into you. The energy and vision you've given me for my book, and future career, well I can't thank you for enough. I'm running with it! Thanks again.*
>
> *Regards*
>
> *Jon*

We all have these moments in our lifetime and if we can stay focused and pay attention to the fingerprint we're leaving, there will be even more!

Can you imagine what sort of a world we would live in if everyone on the planet took this approach? If they intentionally left a positive fingerprint in every brief connection as they went about their day.

The Guest House

BY RUMI

This being human is a guest house.
Every morning a new arrival.

A joy, a depression, a meanness,
some momentary awareness comes
as an unexpected visitor.

Welcome and entertain them all!
Even if they're a crowd of sorrows,
who violently sweep your house
empty of its furniture,
still, treat each guest honourably.
He may be clearing you out
for some new delight.

The dark thought, the shame, the malice,
meet them at the door laughing,
and invite them in.

Be grateful for whoever comes,
because each has been sent
as a guide from beyond.

We don't always look at other people as possible guides to help us see what we need to see and yet Rumi's poem is a reminder that we should see them all as a gift to help us grow. Sometimes the strangers we meet along the way like the young lady in the shop for me, or our kids, or someone else who is close to us is just holding up the mirror and reflecting back to us what we need to get so we can move on in our lives without falling into another hole!

There's an old saying that goes something like: "Get your own house in order before criticising others."

Or this one from the King James Bible: "You hypocrite! First, remove the beam out of your own eye, and then you can see clearly to remove the speck out of your brother's eye."

Two Wolves Story

An old Cherokee is teaching his grandson about life. "A fight is going on inside me," he said to the boy. "It is a terrible fight and it is between two wolves. One is evil – he is anger, envy, sorrow, regret, greed, arrogance, self-pity, guilt, resentment, inferiority, lies, false pride, superiority, and ego."

He continued, "The other is good – he is joy, peace, love, hope, serenity, humility, kindness, benevolence, empathy, generosity, truth, compassion, and faith. The same fight is going on inside you – and inside every other person, too."

The grandson thought about it for a minute and then asked his grandfather, "Which wolf will win?"

The old Cherokee simply replied, "The one you feed."

I'm not sure if the story is true in terms of the origin but it makes the point that throughout our day these two choices are available to us.

If you feed the wolf that represents evil, anger and self-pity it will keep you stuck with low self-confidence and low self-esteem. There is so much additional noise that we can tune into via TV and social media when we are stuck in this way of thinking which only ever feeds the darkness more and more, which in turn pulls you deeper into the darkness.

If you are currently stuck in blaming the world for everything that is showing up in your life right now, it's easy to feed the dark wolf as it helps grow your anger and bitterness towards the world and other people and you end up looking for more evidence to back up your thinking. You end up deleting, distorting and generalising any evidence that doesn't back up your current thinking.

To break this pattern of thinking, you must choose to go against the current flow of your thinking, you must catch yourself and stop for a moment and then get a snack out for the other wolf, the wolf of light who can transform your life for the better. There's a sense of freedom knowing that you actually have a choice moment by moment, especially when a curve ball shows up that you weren't expecting.

Pulling up rice shoots to help them grow

The proverb stems from a story told in Gongsun Chou shang (Gongsun Chou I) by Mencius (372-289 BCE), the most famous Confucian next only to Confucius himself.

Once, in the state of Song, there was an impatient farmer. After he transplanted rice seedlings in the paddy fields, he hoped that they would grow into rice overnight. He came to the fields several times a day to watch the seedlings grow. Of course, the more he watched, the less patient he became. Finally he couldn't help but jump into the muddy fields and started pulling all the seedlings up an inch. He believed that by doing so, he was helping to hasten their growth. When he returned home, his sons were puzzled to see him so exhausted. When asked what he had been doing, he told them that he had been helping the rice shoots to grow. "How?" they asked, and his answer horrified them. Without hesitation, they dashed to the fields, but it was too late: As they had feared, the rice seedlings had already withered.

Meaning: Spoil a thing by being over enthusiastic about it.

Every leader I have ever worked with, have all needed to slow down, I believe we have been fooled into thinking that a fast response is better than a well thought through answer when someone is asking for an opinion on something. Maybe we believe that others will think poorly of us if we don't come back immediately with something clever.

There very rarely is ever an emergency to respond with haste, we need to get better at applying a measured and well thought out plan before we steam ahead. As they say, "patience is a virtue".

> *"The happiness of your life depends upon the quality of your thoughts."*
>
> MARCUS AURELIUS

CHAPTER 10

Bringing it all Together

In December 2017, 10 months after my separation with Tracey, I knew it would be tough spending Christmas by myself in the small garage conversion I had been renting, so I decided to travel to Australia and New Zealand to avoid the isolation. Typically, our Christmas was spent with Tracey's parents on Christmas Day and then on Boxing day we would have a big family gathering with games and activities late into the night.

Going back to where I grew up and seeing my brothers and friends would be a treat. I landed in Oz and spent a few days there visiting friends and family before flying over to New Zealand to stay with Max Pendleton and his girlfriend Sarah. They were great hosts and had their own house in Blenheim and a spare bike I was able to borrow, meaning I was able to join them on their daily rides.

Whilst I was there I was contacted by an athlete and professional rower who was part of the New Zealand rowing team at the height of his rowing career called Craig Harper, who asked if we could meet for a coffee. Craig had just set a new world record for the end-to-end cycle crossing of New Zealand and was looking for his next challenge! He'd been told by a mutual acquaintance that I'd tackled RAAM a few times and wanted to find out more. We got together and had a long conversation about the complexities of RAAM: the number of crew he would need, assigning their roles, sorting out logistics and so on. It was a longer list than he had initially thought. I left Craig suggesting we keep in touch and told him I'd be happy to help if he decided to take part in RAAM at any point in the future.

I left New Zealand and thought no more about it. I was busy with work commitments back in the UK, so I was surprised when Craig emailed me out of the blue to see if we could set up a Skype call to discuss him competing in the 2019 RAAM.

I was happy to help with advice but wasn't sure whether I could afford being away from work for three weeks. As things continued to progress in a positive way for Craig in his quest to get sponsors on board, he started discussing the idea of paying to cover my loss of earnings. It started to become an easy conversation and I offered up my services as a coach to get him in the best possible mindset both for the race and for everything else that was going to come his way during the race and in the build-up to it.

For me this was an opportunity to combine everything I had learnt as a coach with all of my personal insights from trying to run a business, be present with my family and pursue the huge feat of racing a bike across America.

I was in a unique position to help Craig become more aware of being fully present in the decisions he was making and the impact it would have on his family. From my own darkness I would be able to shine some light for Craig to see his own way through achieving his best performance whilst maintaining a balance with his family and business – something I clearly struggled with in both of my marriages. Instead of him going through the school of hard knocks and learning as he went along, I could signpost some of the potential pitfalls and how to either avoid them completely or navigate them more effectively.

The coaching started the same way I begin all of my coaching engagements. I asked Craig to go online and complete an Emotional

Intelligence questionnaire, which comprises 168 questions. It uncovers the patterns of behaviour we run as human beings and creates awareness for the individual around their potential blind spots, along with highlighting their positive behaviours.

In our first coaching session we went through his Emotional Intelligence profile. This was a deep dive and I explored his timeline, with a commentary from Craig about his life to date and all of the experiences that had shaped him so far. After the first session I suggested a reading list for Craig to build and broaden his mindset and challenge some of his beliefs about what he thought was possible for him.

By this stage, I was already on board as his crew chief and we had started having regular calls as the crew continued to grow. Craig was able to hand-pick a highly talented group of people who had in their own right competed at a high level in various sports. Some, like Craig, were from a rowing background, including his wife, Kate, who was part of the NZ rowing team. Others had successful businesses and had been involved in supporting Craig as a cyclist in various large events in New Zealand. All in all, Craig had assembled an excellent team, including his good friend Jason, who was doing a great job with PR and media which took care of the costs of taking part in the race, which is always one of the biggest challenges of doing RAAM.

Through the coaching sessions and the reading list I had given him, Craig continued to build on his already solid mindset and was becoming a more rounded and sensitive human being. His family could see the change and close friends could see his transformation. His purpose altered from solely wanting to compete against the best riders in ultra-cycling to also becoming a role model to inspire others to take part in sport and be better people in life in general.

I know for sure that Craig's growth during the coaching process was significant, he had gone from being a typically driven and self-focused athlete to someone who started being more aware of the impact he was have on others around him, in particular his wife Kate and his daughters

Brooke and Hannah and he extended his positive fingerprint to others that he now encountered as he went about his day.

He improved his flexibility and his ability to connect with others grew as this new version of Craig emerged as a butterfly emerges from a cocoon from the new mindset that he took on from thinking differently about life and racing.

The Race Across America is such an extreme race that it really does take someone special to be able to handle themselves as they cycle the 3,000 miles non-stop with very little sleep. Craig did inspire thousands of people following him online across the world and, more importantly, with the help of Jason's media links was able to inspire people back home in New Zealand, including his two daughters Hannah and Brooke.

Craig ended up finishing fourth overall in the 2019 solo Race Across America. His efforts were supported by an exceptional crew, and even though I thought that we had enough time before the race to get everything sorted, time seemed to evaporate and there was the usual rookie crew mayhem for the first 48 hours before we settled into a pattern that seemed to work as the race unfolded.

Even with crews that have been across a few times, it's never smooth, and we had our share of bumps across the team. Lack of sleep has such an impact on decision-making and simple math turns into complex algebra! Keeping track of the route changes becomes difficult and navigating errors are easily made. All in all, though, we got Craig across the finish line safely and without any time penalties. As a first-timer he was delighted with his performance.

On reflection, I realised that there's not a lot to be gained by trying to unpick all of the various problems and issues we had as a crew, who was to blame for that wrong turn or didn't have that bit of kit ready on time. One of the guys, Callum, mentioned that he was very good at picking at a scab when something didn't work out the way he might have hoped and I saw that this was something we needed to avoid.

It's always easy to expect perfection and set the bar too high – and a lot harder to achieve.

Being an old hand at this by now, I know that the team performed remarkably well. By the end of Craig's race we were all completely spent and dazed. We celebrated with a mid-morning breakfast, during which half of us fell asleep whilst sipping on a beer to celebrate our collective achievement! That in itself shows that we were all completely knackered and that we all put everything into supporting Craig. He in turn laid his heart and soul across America, and from an athletic perspective he gave his all. It was a privilege to see it all, from first meeting Craig in Blenheim to the RAAM finish line.

"Be yourself, everyone else is already taken."

CHAPTER 11

A Happy Ending

Here's the painful truth: there is no happy ending in this story so far! What I know for sure is that history has taught us all that we're not getting out of this alive. We're born, we live our lives and we die. I know it might come across as harsh but that's the truth. Sorry if I'm bursting your bubble but that's the gig.

It's what you do with this stark reminder that can absolutely transform your life in a very positive way. I guess at some point you've got to ask yourself whether you are truly living a full life or are you taking each day for granted?

So, the fairytale can be real if you are able to live every day to your fullest potential and the only way to do that is to be fully engaged in whatever you are doing moment by moment each and every day. You'll be living your dream one moment at a time and each of those separate moments you are consciously spending your life force on whatever it is that you are doing.

Was there a moment when I had a deep realisation that I had gotten it horribly wrong? It all became very real that the patterns I had created weren't working for me and my relationships when Tracey asked me to leave our family house and that she couldn't go on any more as a couple.

Over the next few months through the blur of the dehydrated headache you get from too many tears, I slowly started to realise that this was real and I had to try and piece it all together.

If life is a race, I had to look at how to play it properly and ensure I paid attention to what others' expectations were of me at a deeper level than I had previously explored.

The pain I was causing her had become unbearable and she felt that it would be better for me to be out her life and the family. That was her belief and our beliefs are driven by the pain/pleasure principle, every decision we make is linked to pain or pleasure!

I had paid the ultimate price by competing in 3 solo RAAM races, I lost the woman I loved and the extended family by running a number of patterns that didn't serve us as a couple, I didn't really see this until I was on the outside looking back at what had happened. Like a forensic detective, I was only able to see this when I pieced it all together.

The way we dress ourselves to go out into the world is linked to whether you'll look good in your choice of clothes or not, every aspect of what we do is locked into this pattern. How you get your haircut, the food you eat is a pain/pleasure decision, will this take me towards my goal of staying healthy and fit or do I not care? So much of this pattern is hidden under the surface of every choice we make.

I know for sure that I allowed myself to stay stuck for a good couple of years believing that I didn't deserve to be happy or successful in whatever I was pursuing.

What I've come to recognise for myself through therapy is that the whole breakdown of any relationship is a two-way thing and that it's more about how I respond to the pain of the significant change that took place when the line was drawn on that part of my life. As a coach I can hear myself offering up advice about others not taking on board other people's opinions of themselves, and yet I had to accept that I had made some mistakes and this has helped me to learn and grow, and I will ensure that I don't make the same mistakes in the future.

So, what am I going to do about it? Well, all I can do is to use these experiences to grow and help others see the possible patterns they are running in their own lives. I will do everything I can to continue to build strong relationships with all of my kids and keep a keen eye on any potential destructive patterns.

We all have a filing cabinet that we carry around with us throughout our lives, it's full of all of our memories – good and bad. For most of us, the filing cabinet gets weighed down by all of the unhappy events. For some reason, we can readily recall all of the drama which keeps us stuck in that little black raincloud that seems to follow us around. It's one of the reasons that I keep a journal to remind myself of the highlights during my day. I tend to use my journal as a reflective tool by asking myself three questions: 1. What worked well today or what were my wins? 2. What did I learn about myself or others? 3. What do I need to change about myself or how I go about things differently next time?

Simply put, it's called Win, Learn, Change and is a powerful way of ensuring you get incremental improvement in whatever you're doing.

Something I picked up from reading was a lovely idea of getting everyone in your family to write down their highlight of that week on a Post-it note and place it in a container and to then open it up on New Year's Eve and read them to each other. You can even use different colours for each family member. There is evidence that making a note of the things you are grateful for on a regular basis boosts your immune system and overall well-being. Neuroscience is now catching up with a lot of the actual benefits of keeping a journal. Logically it adds up that keeping score and reviewing everything that is going well will have a positive impact, so it becomes a no-brainer.

Our destiny gets shaped when we make a decision. For a lot of people, myself included, we get distracted away from pursuing our goals because other aspects of our lives get in the way and derail us. I've defaulted on a number of occasions where I've told myself I'll start it tomorrow or next week or next month and we all know where that ends up going!

I've already spoken about the ABC of Success and it's the "C" which is the thing that catches me out whenever I don't finish a goal or task I'm chasing. It's the "commitment" to seeing it all the way to completion that can trip us up.

The struggle is part of the journey

This story is a great reminder for all of us about the various curve balls that show up in our lives and our opportunity for growth if we can see them as just that, an opportunity to stretch and grow through the struggles. At the time it doesn't always look like an opportunity, but if we look deep enough we can find some real gems through the adversity.

Once a little boy was playing outdoors and found a fascinating caterpillar. He carefully picked it up and took it home to show his mother. He asked his mother if he could keep it, and she said he could if he would take good care of it.

The little boy got a large jar from his mother and put plants for the caterpillar to eat, and a stick to climb on, in the jar. Every day he watched the caterpillar and brought it new plants to eat.

One day the caterpillar climbed up the stick and started acting strangely. The boy worriedly called his mother, who understood that the caterpillar was creating a cocoon. The mother explained to the boy how the caterpillar was going to go through a metamorphosis and become a butterfly.

The little boy was thrilled to hear about the changes his caterpillar would go through. He watched every day, waiting for the butterfly to emerge. One day it happened, a small hole appeared in the cocoon and the butterfly started to struggle to come out.

At first the boy was excited, but soon he became concerned. The butterfly was struggling so hard to get out! It looked like it couldn't break free! It looked desperate! It looked like it was making no progress!

The boy was so concerned he decided to help. He got some scissors and snipped the cocoon to make the hole bigger and the butterfly quickly emerged!

As the butterfly came out the boy was surprised. It had a swollen body and small, shrivelled wings. He continued to watch the butterfly expecting that, at any moment, the wings would dry out, enlarge and expand to support the swollen body. He knew that in time the body would shrink and the butterfly's wings would expand.

But neither happened!

The butterfly spent the rest of its life crawling around with a swollen body and shrivelled wings.

It never was able to fly...

As the boy tried to figure out what had gone wrong his mother took him to talk to a scientist from a local college. He learned that the butterfly was SUPPOSED to struggle. In fact, the butterfly's struggle to push its way through the tiny opening of the cocoon pushes the fluid out of its body and into its wings. Without the struggle, the butterfly would never, ever fly. The boy's good intentions hurt the butterfly.

As you go through school, and life, keep in mind that struggling is an important part of any growth experience. In fact, it is the struggle that causes you to develop your ability to fly.

"Change is never painful, only resistance to change is painful."

BUDDHA

I'm not flying yet but I've found my wings again and I'm certainly out of my cocoon from my past couple of years of being stuck. I'm ready to fully live every day and ensure that I greet everyone I meet with love in my heart and to stay curious.

This is not just about relationships. We can all get stuck with having to pay the bills and sometimes feel overwhelmed when it seems as though you're not winning or making any progress, but, as the above story suggests, it's all part of the journey to a better, stronger version of yourself.

I remember having a conversation with my eldest daughter Megan some years ago about how at the time she was stressed about various things in her life. We were walking along the beach in Bournemouth and I stopped her and asked her to look out at the sea. In particular, I asked Megan to look at the waves and as she started to pay attention to the patterns they made she noticed that they tended to come in sets. Some of the waves were a foot or so in height and some were a lot larger. As she noticed this, I mentioned that life was a bit like this as well.

We can all handle the small waves and can get used to not being too bothered by them, but every now and then a much larger wave has the potential to knock us off our feet. We know that when we do get knocked down by one of those big ones, it's critical to pick ourselves back up and be ready for the next set of waves.

There will always be curve balls or waves in our lives that can knock us down, but what shapes us is how we respond to that adversity. Unfortunately, some people stay down when they get bowled over and they end up getting stuck. That's where family and friends are so important. We need to get better at asking for help before we spiral out of control.

When pursuing a goal of any kind, I find that breaking the goal down into smaller chunks helps me take stock of where I am. I can then check my progress as the weeks skip by. I've shared my handprint process from my coaching practice at the end of the book to help you to set your goals and then chunk them down.

The quote below is one of my favourites as it speaks to an aspect of why I've always wanted to test myself. I've been very open with some of the hidden reasons of what compelled me to push myself but within this quote is a key element that lights my desire to get involved and test myself, whether that's working with a tricky group of leaders or being a better father to my kids.

> *"It is not the critic who counts; not the man who points out how the strong man stumbles, or where the doer of deeds could have done them better. The credit belongs to the man who is actually in the arena, whose face is marred by dust and sweat and blood; who strives valiantly; who errs, who comes short again and again, because there is no effort without error and shortcoming; but who does actually strive to do the deeds; who knows great enthusiasms, the great devotions; who spends himself in a worthy cause; who at the best knows in the end the triumph of high achievement, and who at the worst, if he fails, at least fails while daring greatly, so that his place shall never be with those cold and timid souls who neither know victory nor defeat."*

THEODORE ROOSEVELT

I don't mind being judged because it's something we all do. I was never scared to put myself on the start line of various ultra-races because unconsciously I felt that I was attempting to show my inner child that everything would be OK. In turn, I've paid ultimate price of losing the woman I loved and dented some of the relationships with my kids.

I know for sure that I've learnt so much from uncovering some of my Vicious Cycles and I hope I've shed enough light on some of my darkness in my journey so far, which in turn will benefit you in your life in a good way. And that you can take some learning and create a deeper awareness of your own patterns, which will allow you to grow and leave a more positive fingerprint with everyone you interact with from now on.

I've decided that I'm perfectly imperfect and that's OK!

In the speech that Sylvester Stallone gave his son in the Rocky Balboa movie that he wrote, produced and acted in. Rocky delivers the talk to his son at a time when his son is on his knees and gets caught up in blaming everything around himself and even blames Rocky for the troubles he's facing in his life.

Rocky challenges his son to take personal responsibility and go out and create the future life he wants and not allow anyone or anything to take that away from him. It's a speech all parents need to instill in their children when they're ready to hear it.

The speech reminds his son that life can be tough at times but it's more about how you respond to the things that happen, which in turn moulds you into who you become.

I've managed to turn some of my poor patterns around completely as I did the hard yards to focus on creating better habits around my relationships and finances, my fitness has never really been an issue for me and I continue to compete in Ironman races around the world.

I CAN'T

When faced with a difficulty that I can see

My immediate thought is I can't, that's just me

How much do I limit my potential with this small word

Maybe if I make it smaller, it won't be heard

Can't stops me from so many things

Stops me from looking at what life brings

The chances you take can be stopped by can't

There should be no limitations, there just aren't

I'm going to scrub this word from my mind

And open new doors and seek and find

I can do anything if I erase the letter "T"

I know I need to, it's up to me.

JIM REES

*"Give a man a fish, and you feed him
for a day. Teach a man to fish, and you
feed him for a lifetime."*

MAIMONIDES

O U T R O

Covid-19

Having worked with thousands of people as a coach, I have learnt that we will always be faced with what I call "curve balls" in our lives. These events can be personal to us or extend to our whole family or beyond our family to our business, communities and country.

Prior to Covid-19, most people in the UK were in a state of anxiety about Brexit and then due to the global pandemic, Brexit almost became a non-event. Covid has been a global curve ball affecting millions of families and businesses across the world. I've seen first-hand how leaders have attempted to navigate this with the information that they have from their governments.

How they continue to handle themselves throughout this pandemic will have two extreme outcomes: they will either handle it with great empathy and compassion, which will create a great deal of emotional collateral and their teams will walk on hot coals for them; or they will display a lack of engagement and trust will be eroded completely. In this situation people will be looking at everything you do as a leader more than ever before and they will be less forgiving.

When we come out of the other side of Covid and things start to settle into a new rhythm there will be other curve balls we will need to deal with. What I'm talking about here, in essence, is how we handle change.

Most of us, myself included, struggle with change; yet change is a constant.

We need to take a different look at change and remind ourselves that it's natural, the seasons help us see this, day and night is a reminder of the constant flow. Our bodies over three months regenerate just about every cell, which means there's a new version of ourselves every quarter! We don't really see these subtle changes but change is something that we can rely upon. What we struggle with is how we handle the change. The neuroscientist Dr Andrew Huberman has spoken about the next step for human evolution, which is all about managing our state more effectively. Unfortunately, due to over-stimulation from technology we have become hyper-sensitive to our environment and are increasingly less able to manage our mental and physical state.

Our brain helps us filter millions of bits of information every second, which helps us not to have to think about when we need to take our next breath and automatically runs our whole body. Various areas of the brain take care of logic, emotion and our motor skills. But where we have become overwhelmed is in the part of the brain known as the amygdala. It's often referred to as the reptilian brain and, very simply, it's responsible for fight or flight. Back in caveman and cavewoman days this part of the brain protected us, telling us whenever a predator came too close whether to run away or stand our ground. Nowadays, as we are bombarded by phone calls, texts, emails, social media, and TV, our brain has become over-loaded. When we see negative stories on the TV or in the press, or when we receive negative emails or get into online disagreements with other people on social media our amygdala struggles with how to handle the situation. Do we fight? And if so, who do we fight? And how? Or do we run away? And where do we run to? All the while and in response to this bombardment, our brains are producing chemical cascades of adrenaline and cortisol that we are unable to work off by physically tackling our virtual "predator" or running away from it. This being so, those harmful, over-stimulating chemicals remain in our system as a kind of poison.

This is one reason why Mindfulness has become so popular. It's a way we can detox from the stress and anxiety that daily modern life induces in us.

Covid has awoken millions of people, forcing them to question how they've been running their lives: do we really need to commute 1-2 hours every day; can we be more productive working from home? Prior to Covid, this way of working went unquestioned. It was "normal" but was it "good".

I've heard so many stories of how being forced to work from home has given people a deeper connection to their families, and has helped them to maintain healthier and fitter lifestyles. What they have gained, above all, is time. It's the most important commodity any of us has and we need to use it wisely. All the material and financial things we are conditioned to chase can't buy us more time with our loved ones. It's taken a global pandemic for most of the world to realise this, and it will be interesting to see how many people return to their old ways of life – voluntarily or not – once the Covid crisis is over.

My hope is that we as a species will wake up from this slumber and start acting and behaving as a collective with love and compassion in our hearts for all beings – human and otherwise. In turn, this will help us to protect our planet for future generations. It's in our hands.

*"A journey of a thousand miles starts
with a single step."*

AFTERWORD

The Final Say by Craig Harper

People say you need to make the most of opportunities. Some people sit still and reply that they aren't lucky – there is no opportunity coming for them. I have always believed that opportunities don't come along dressed up nicely in a package; you actually need to go searching for them. They take effort to put yourself in position and they require you to follow through with action. The very best opportunities are the ones that happen unexpectedly. Or, better still, unknowingly at the time.

I first met Jim Rees in 2017 by chance, when a friend of a friend mentioned he was holidaying in my hometown of Blenheim in New Zealand and there might be a chance to meet up. It was all very quick and I was caught in the middle of a busy day with work, so it took some effort to arrange the time to go and meet him.

I did not know Jim, but I heard he was a multiple finisher from RAAM, the race I had followed for a few years and been fascinated with its iconic challenges. It's fair to say I had dreamed of doing it, but was unsure how to go about organising the mammoth logistical challenge from my side of the world where ultra-cycling is almost unheard of.

Something told me that this was an introduction not to be missed, so I rushed away from work and met Jim over a coffee. Initially it was the intrigue in learning more about RAAM that dragged me to the café. As a result, it was an almost two-hour coffee break, as we discussed cycling (ultra-distance of course), and a bit about ourselves.

And so began an epic 18-month journey. A journey that has taught me so much about myself, my relationship with people, and how to get the best out of what I do. The journey came to a fairytale ending on 22 June 2019, when I crossed the finish line of RAAM at City Dock, Annapolis, MD.

After that chance meeting with Jim, he agreed to help me prepare for my race. We started frequent online meetings where we would discuss what lay ahead for me as a rider. I was not new to ultra-distance cycling but I was certainly not hugely experienced, having only done a handful of shorter races in New Zealand with my biggest achievement being my successful length of the country record attempt in 2017 (2,150km in 4 days and 9 hours).

Under Jim's guidance, it soon became apparent to me the most important aspect would be my state of mind. Of course, I needed to do the training on the bike, but an area that I had not previously spent much time in improving was the strength of my mental game. To Jim, it was obvious I had a desire to achieve. But the will alone of a person needs something else; it needs to be pointed in the right direction if it is to be effective. The catalyst for uniting my team and kickstarting my campaign was the development of a meaningful purpose. Jim helped me shape my purpose and taught me the importance of having something so strong that it comes before all else. In reflection, this purpose I stated at the beginning did two things. Firstly, it made me more self-aware. The more we can act as knowledgeable individuals amongst our friends, family and peers, the better we will be. I was able to look at myself from a third person perspective and consider things more meaningfully than I had initially. Secondly, it gave our team unity and meaning. By declaring a strong purpose aloud to my peers, we were suddenly united with mutual understanding and expectations.

As my months of training and preparation ticked by, Jim and I continued to discuss various books, ideas, and strategies for my campaign, called SOLO.kiwi. My support team consisted of seven fellow Kiwis, Jim, and fellow Brit Mel. We all met online frequently to develop our race logistics and crew operations. Only people who have been involved in RAAM can appreciate the importance of a strong support crew. The rider hands overall responsibility to their crew and the success of the rider largely comes down to the effectiveness of the team.

When it came to the race, Jim took the role as Crew Chief. Despite our geographical challenges as a crew, I feel we prepared as a team very well. Jim allowed my NZ crew members to use their strength of experience with me personally to the team's benefit. His empathy and experience allowed this rookie team to establish its own identity. While the American organisers like to play on the importance of the Crew Chief in all its fanfare, us Kiwis tend to prefer less attention and do the job required without external glory. Jim acknowledged this, and while he brought leadership and learnings from his experiences when needed, he also allowed us to act as a rookie crew with pride and quiet confidence. In reflection of the knowledge I have learnt throughout this journey, Jim and I are the same but also very different. I owe Jim a lot for what I have learnt and for the person I have become.

We have both given ourselves the unique opportunity to call ourselves RAAM solo finishers. How we got there, though, seems very different. Maybe we have experienced different circles at different times? When I hear of Jim's childhood struggles and vicious emotional circles, I can only feel grateful for the love and support I received as a young boy (that continues to this day). As a father in my family now, I am more aware of than ever of the importance of this love and presence. Aside from the circle you experience, it is also true that age brings wisdom. Some would agree that after finishing RAAM you feel 20 years older, so I guess I'm a whole lot wiser, and Jim is much wiser still! We all face fears though, no matter how strong or wise we are. The aspect Jim preaches about fear is very true.

"And as we let our own light shine,
We unconsciously give other people
permission to do the same.
As we are liberated from our own fear, our
presence automatically liberates others."

I have never analysed an adventure (or failure) with as much thought as I have about RAAM. People close to me have commented that I have changed along the journey. I'd agree in that I feel more enriched because of the people I've connected with, the way I responded to challenges, the willingness I now have for more challenges, and an understanding of metacognitive thinking.

These skills as well as others were developed in my training with Jim in the months prior to RAAM. They allowed me to form an effective team around me and overcome the ups and downs through such a consuming journey. It is difficult to explain RAAM. The challenges are endless and are on different scales to different people, depending on their experience, knowledge and resources. But it is not limited to just the individual. There is no other solo event that relies so heavily on the racer's support crew as much as RAAM. While the racer is faced with obvious and extreme physical challenges, there are many time, logistical, navigational and practical difficulties the crew must also handle out of a moving vehicle, 24 hours a day. I think for a rookie racer, the most dictating (and controllable) factor is self-belief. The 12-day race cut-off for solos is ruthless. But is also very achievable with willpower. The truth is, once you have been riding for four days non-stop, it doesn't really matter how fit or strong a rider you are (don't get me wrong – physical condition is important and can dictate whether you may finish in eight or 11 days). What matters most is the ability to keep moving. Even slow progress is progress and, sometimes, when you feel like you are not making any progress, you are actually making the most.

I try to explain to people how achievable races like RAAM actually are and I get some strange looks. These are people who may have never had the courage to attempt something risky. Or maybe they don't understand the benefits in actually seeking discomfort. I try to explain that having the courage to step outside of your comfort zone can be very empowering. Not being dictated to by your fears, not being dictated by other people, in my mind is true courage. This feeling you get when you are courageous enough to follow through is, in essence, a RAAM racer's WHY.

Since RAAM, with the knowledge Jim helped me discover, I have enjoyed sharing my experiences. Public speaking and the like is not something that comes naturally to me, but I now understand the reason the above quotation about fear is valuable. I know that the light I found, and fears I overcame, actually inspired and uplifted others. People I did not know. People who knew nothing about RAAM and ultra-cycling. At first this surprised me, but I now accept it with pride. Through cycling I have been able to find something that sparks me up and challenges me physically as well as mentally. I can only encourage people to find their "something" which not only lights them up but which also questions their fears. Be courageous and you will experience a much richer life. To Jim, THANK YOU for leaving your positive fingerprint on my life. I only hope I can do the same for others. Kia Kaha.

Oh, one final story so that you really get my point about pursuing your inner greatness.

The Eagle and the Chicken

There's an old, well-known story of a chicken farmer who found an eagle's egg.

He put it with his chickens and soon the egg hatched.

The young eagle grew up with all the other chickens and whatever they did, the eagle did too. He thought he was a chicken, just like them.

Since the chickens could only fly for a short distance, the eagle also learnt to fly a short distance.

He thought that was what he was supposed to do. So that was all that he thought he could do. As a consequence, that was all he was able to do.

One day the eagle saw a bird flying high above him. He was very impressed. "Who is that?" he asked the hens around him.

"That's the eagle, the king of the birds," the hens told him. "He belongs to the sky. We belong to the earth, we are just chickens."

So the eagle lived and died as a chicken, for that's what he thought he was.

I want to encourage you today that you are an eagle.

You may have been brought up in a situation that limited your understanding of your potential, but it's time now for the past to lose its hold on you.

Don't die thinking you're a chicken.

Soar high, just as you were meant to.

Be all that you are meant to be and tap into your inner greatness that has always been there. With love and light Jim

VALUES EXERCISE

Looking Backward

Take yourself to the end of your life. The truth, good or bad, is there.

Now get a pen. Rank in order on the left from 1 - 10 the values you most want your life to reflect, 1 being the highest value and 10 being the least valued. This is your vision, the most personal of visions and how you want to be remembered.

	Wealth (the amount of money you have)	
	Material possessions (how much stuff you've acquired)	
	Family & friends (however you define it)	
	Social status (job titles, degrees, awards)	
	Health (spiritual, physical, mental, and emotional)	
	Power (how many people you lead)	
	Ethical character (your expression towards others of love, kindness, honesty, generosity, gratitude, etc)	
	Fame (how many people know you)	
	Appearance (the importance of looking good)	
	Performance at work (your competence and mastery)	

Now consider the time and energy you've invested over the last several years, and rank these values on the right hand side from 1 - 10 based on how much time and energy you've actually invested in each. Once finished, take a look at any differences in your scores to see where you need to pay attention to close any gaps.

THE HANDPRINT GOAL SETTING MODEL

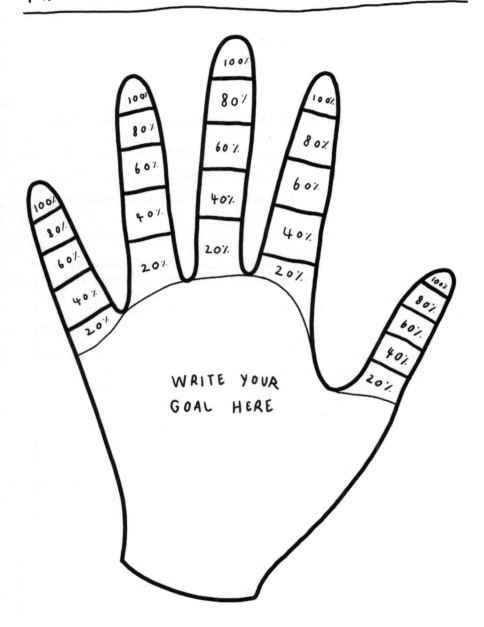

Handprint instructions:-

Get a blank A4 piece of paper and trace around your non dominant hand. Close off the bottom of the palm as seen in the diagram, then draw 4 lines across each finger and thumb and add the percentage figures 20%, 40% , 60% , 80% , 100%.

Write your goal in the centre of the palm.

Now ask yourself, what are the five things that are critical to help you achieve your goal? Write these points at the top of each finger.

Once you've done that, you now need to shade in each percentage point you are towards achieving your goal right now? In a lot of cases, this could end up being 0% because you haven't done anything yet on that particular point.

Now you will have a clear visual representation of where you are right now in terms of achieving your goal.

The next step is to take each finger point and create 5 more handprints using the topic from each of the individual fingers.

The question you need to ask yourself now is: what 5 things do I need to do to get this to 100%? Then, add a timeframe of when you want to achieve this by.

When you have fully shaded in your handprint, you will have achieved your goal.

Recommended further reading:-

The 4 Agreements by Don Miguel Ruiz

5 People You Meet in Heaven by Mitch Albom

Leadership and Self Deception by The Abridger Institute

Mindset by Carol Dweck

Breaking the Habit of Being Yourself by Joe Dispenza

Radical Forgiveness by Colin Tipping

Emotional Intelligence at Work (How to Make Change Stick) by Dr Jo Maddocks

The Alchemist by Paulo Coelho

The Charge by Brendon Burchard

Atomic Habits by James Clear

Chasing Daylight by Eugene O'Kelly

The Divine Matrix by Greg Brandon

There is a spiritual solution to every problem by Wayne Dyer

Grit by Angela Duckworth

Can't Hurt Me by David Goggins

A New Earth by Eckhart Tolle

Triggers by Marshall Goldsmith

Loving What Is by Byron Katie

The Biology of Beliefs by Bruce Lipton

Other books by Jim Rees:

All books can be ordered via Amazon

Maximise Your Mind-power
a handbook looking at Mindset strategies.

A Quick Guide to Emotional Intelligence
a short guide to understanding EI.

Built for Greatness
an inspirational book of quotes with the authors view of what they mean in todays world.